I0814210

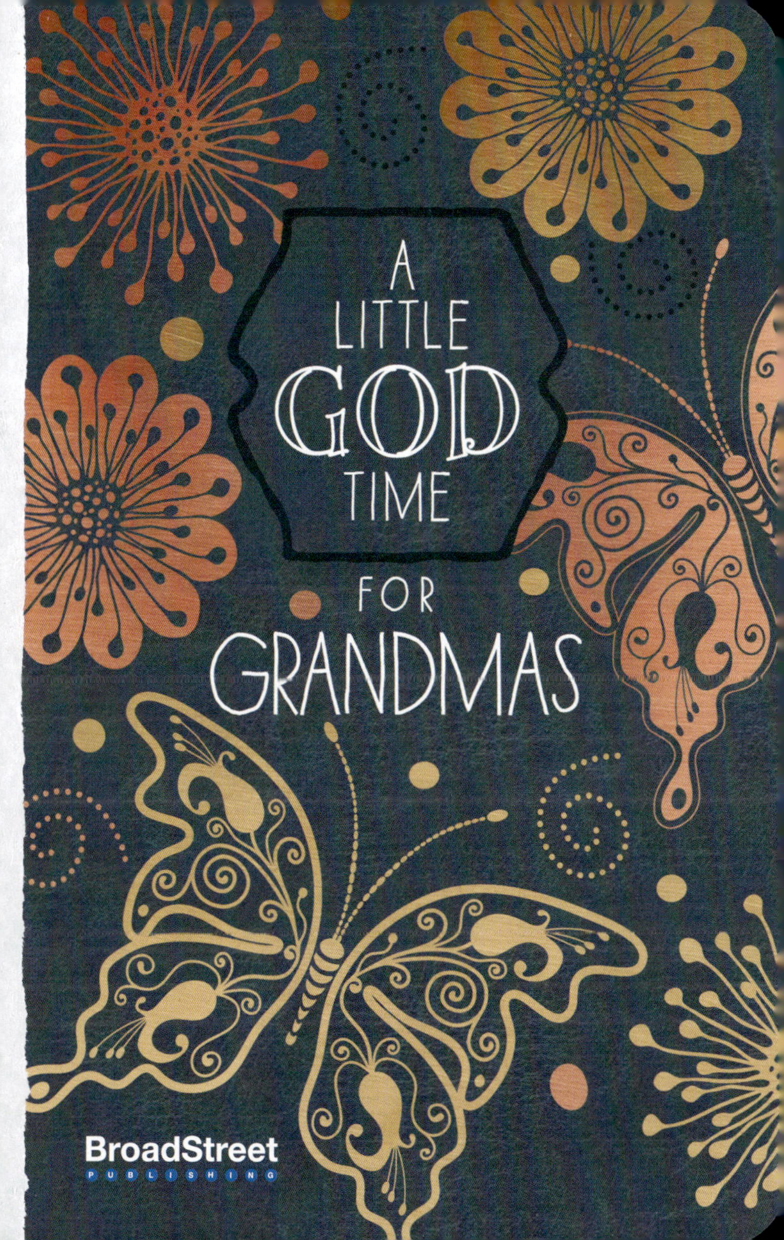
A
LITTLE
GOD
TIME
FOR
GRANDMAS
BroadStreet
PUBLISHING

BroadStreet Publishing Group, LLC.
Savage, Minnesota, USA
Broadstreetpublishing.com

A LITTLE GOD TIME FOR GRANDMAS

9781424566952
9781424566969 (eBook)

Devotional entries composed by Suzanne Niles.

Typesetting and design by Garborg Design Works | garborgdesign.com
Editorial services by Michelle Winger | literallyprecise.com and Natasha Marcellus

Printed in China.

25 26 27 28 29 30 31 7 6 5 4 3 2 1

One generation commends
your works to another;
they tell of your mighty acts.

Psalm 145:4 NIV

INTRODUCTION

If grandmothers ran the world, grandkids would always be within arms' reach—at least until Grandma needed a little quiet time to relax and recharge. But life doesn't work that way. Even if you live right around the corner, your grown children—and their children—lead busy lives. Spending time together may not be for as long or frequent as your heart wishes it would be.

Make the most of the time you have, together or apart, by drawing closer to God and to your grandkids. As you spend a little God time reading these daily devotions, Scriptures, and prayers, you will be inspired to put your love into action, whether in person or on your knees.

Celebrate the unparalleled blessings that being a grandmother brings as you are strengthened and encouraged by the one who loves your grandchildren more than you ever could. And that is saying something!

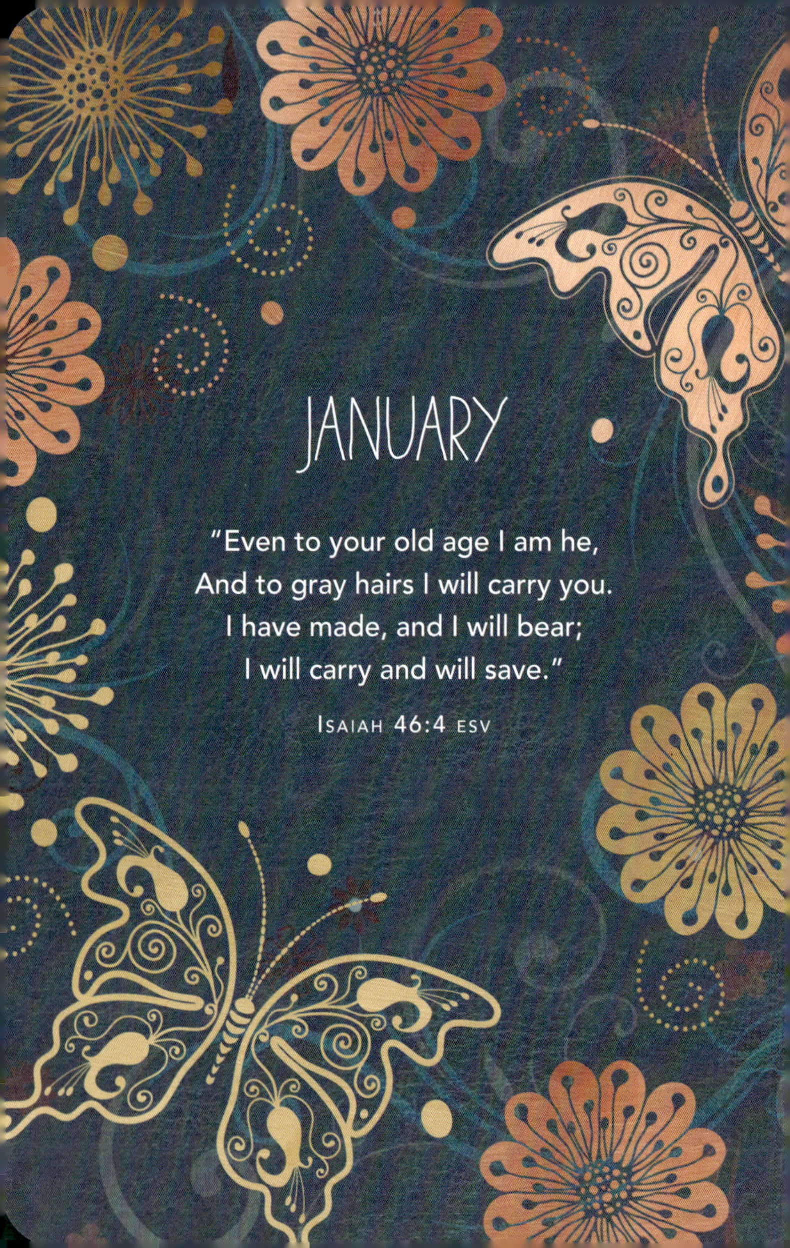

JANUARY

"Even to your old age I am he,
And to gray hairs I will carry you.
I have made, and I will bear;
I will carry and will save."

Isaiah 46:4 ESV

THOUGHTS OF YOU

Every time I think of you,
I give thanks to my God.

PHILIPPIANS 1:3 NLT

As grandparents we know the burst of joy in our hearts when we see our grandbabies. It's a delight to be able to enjoy this season of life. The privilege of being called *Grandma* stirs up thanksgiving and acts as a reminder to praise God for the gift of each precious child.

Next time you find yourself filled with delight at the thought of your grandchildren, remember that your heavenly Father looks at you with great pride as well. You are his masterpiece and not a second goes by that you aren't on his mind. Just as you hope your grandchildren will know the depth of your love for them, God wants you to know how greatly he delights in you.

Thank you, Father, for rejoicing over me as one of your precious children! I'm thankful for your kindness and affection.

SEEK WISDOM

Their purpose is to teach people
to live disciplined and successful lives,
to help them do what is right, just, and fair.

PROVERBS 1:3 NLT

With each year that passes, we step further away from our own childbearing days. Sometimes, as that gap grows, we might forget some of the stresses that come with raising young children. It's easy to look at a young parent and assume that we could do better. Instead of relying on our own experiences and opinions, we should encourage our children to look to the wisdom of scripture for parenting help.

Remember that your child will struggle to parent just like you did. As they seek to love, teach, and discipline their children, your support is incredibly significant. Point them toward Scripture and encourage them to seek wisdom in all that they do.

Father, I ask you to give my children your strength and patience as they train their children. Help them to seek wisdom consistently.

KEEP PRAYING

I have no greater joy than to hear
that my children are walking in the truth.

3 John 1:4 ESV

We all have hopes and dreams for our children. We imagine what type of person they'll be, what they'll accomplish and where they might live. The same is true for each of our grandchildren. Watching them grow and build lives of their own is a great delight. Even greater is the joy that comes from watching them live in a way that honors the Lord.

Pray continuously that your grandchildren will spend their lives seeking Jesus. All your other hopes and dreams for your family don't compare to the great satisfaction that comes from watching them live in the truth. If your grandchildren love the Lord, praise him! If they are far from him, lean on God's promises and trust in his unfailing faithfulness.

Father, I surrender my grandchildren to your hands. I trust that you will be gracious with them and teach them to follow you.

FAMILY FAITH

I think of your strong faith that was passed down through your family line. It began with your grandmother Lois, who passed it on to your dear mother, Eunice. And it's clear that you too are following in the footsteps of their godly example.

2 TIMOTHY 1:5 TPT

Having grandchildren allows us to relive some precious moments. First words, first steps, birthdays and school celebrations all feel extra sweet the second time around. Loving our grandchildren well means sharing that joy as well as sharing the wisdom that we've gleaned from already doing it once. We can encourage and disciple our grandchildren with grace and leave a legacy that honors the Lord.

You have the privilege of passing your faith down to your grandchildren. There might be times you find yourself leaning into the fun parts of being a grandmother while shying away from what seems harder. If you ask, God will faithfully give you the grace to teach your grandchildren about who he is.

Lord, help me to embrace all aspects of being a grandma. I want to share in my children's joy and be faithful to support them as parents.

FREELY GIVEN

If any of you lacks wisdom, he should ask God—
who gives to all generously and ungrudgingly—
and it will be given to him.

JAMES 1:5 CSB

We all remember parenting days when we were at our wits end. We pleaded with God to help us raise our children because we knew that we couldn't do it on our own. When we were in the trenches of conflict and growth, it was easy to be aware of our need for God. Now, as a grandparent years later, it can be tempting to think that we know what is best.

Your need for God is just as great as it has always been! Just because your children are grown doesn't mean that your dependence on the Lord should lessen. He is the one who gives you the grace to be a loving and kind grandmother. Remember to ask him for help! No matter what situation you are in as a grandparent, there is a solution that honors the Lord. Go to him with the expectation that he will give you wisdom.

Father, help me seek you when I need wisdom. I want to honor you as a grandmother.

DILIGENT PRAYERS

Rest in God alone, my soul,
for my hope comes from him.

Psalm 62:5 CSB

It can be heart wrenching to watch our children struggle to parent. We've been there before and know how difficult some days can be. As grandparents, we have the privilege of taking our knowledge and understanding and running to Jesus. We can advocate for our children like no one else can. We can intercede for them when they are overwhelmed by the day-to-day demands of raising children.

When your kids have rough parenting days, don't be discouraged. Take your concerns to the Lord and then rest, knowing that your heavenly Father loves your children and grandchildren more than you do. Just as he is with you, he is establishing his perfect will in their lives.

Father, teach me how to pray for my children and grandchildren. Help me to rest knowing you are in control.

LISTEN AND LEARN

Wise people can also listen and learn;
even they can find good advice in these words.

PROVERBS 1:5 NCV

We all love being right. It's completely normal to think that we know best and that our opinions should be listened to. Problems arise when the satisfaction of being right is greater than the satisfaction that comes from listening to God's opinion. As grandparents, we can spend our days encouraging our children to listen to us or we can encourage them to listen to God.

There will never be a point in your life when you are done listening. The Word says that listening and learning is a mark of wisdom. When you approach life with humility, no matter your age or experience, you honor the Lord. Seek to have a humble heart. Your children and your children's children will reap the rewards.

Father, help me to listen well. Your opinion matters more than my own. Help me to embrace humility.

GOD'S FAITHFULNESS

Being confident of this very thing, that He who has begun a good work in you will complete it until the day of Jesus Christ.

PHILIPPIANS 1:6 NKJV

God will not accomplish in one day what is supposed to take a lifetime. He knows exactly how to lead each of us on the path to being more like himself. As parents we have seen this firsthand with our own children. We've watched them fail and succeed, all in the timing of the Lord. We have seen him begin and finish many good works in the lives of our loved ones.

Don't forget this when it comes to your grandchildren. Give your children the gift of patience and steadfastness. Don't worry or fret when they have parenting struggles. Instead, trust that God is working in them just as he has in your own life. Go to him in prayer and ask him to give you confidence in his ability to bear fruit in their lives.

Father, help me to remember that you will finish everything that you have started. I know that my children and grandchildren are in your hands.

HE SEES

The LORD will watch over your coming and going both now and forevermore.

PSALM 121:8 NIV

The world feels quite different than it did when we were parenting our own young children. As time goes by and the cultural atmosphere shifts, we might long for what seemed like simpler, more innocent days. It can be tempting to fall into the trap of worry and anxiety. We might start to ask ourselves how our grandchildren can possibly thrive in a culture that is so selfish, dark, and overwhelming.

If you feel stress rising due to the world your grandchildren live in, remember who your God is. Prayerfully commit your grandchildren to the Lord. He watched over you and your children faithfully. He will do the same for your grandchildren as they grow. He knows every detail of their days. You can find peace knowing that he was in control then, and he is in control now. Nothing that truly matters has changed.

Thank you, Father, for watching over my loved ones. I know that you are in control.

EYES ON JESUS

The LORD is good,
a strong refuge when trouble comes.
He is close to those who trust in him.

NAHUM 1:7 NLT

As parents, we vividly remember the days of caring for sick children. The nights seemed endless, and worry threatened to take over. Especially in the early years, we all fumbled around a bit, learning how to best take care of our kids. We needed all the support and encouragement we could get.

When your grandchildren are sick, remember the tenderness of those days. Give your children the gift of patience and a steady faith. Pray for them as parents and offer to help however they might need. Remember what it was like to feel unsure and show your children that they can lean on God when they are overwhelmed. You can support them, but God is the one who is their true refuge.

Father, thank you for your unconditional love and constant care. Help me to teach my children how to rely on you as a steady and reliable helper.

GIFT OF DISCIPLESHIP

"I am the Alpha and the Omega," says the Lord God, "who is, and who was, and who is to come, the Almighty."

Revelation 1:8 NIV

It is never too early to train up a child and reveal to them that God is mighty, all-powerful, and sovereign. When they know who God is, they won't be fooled by the lies of the world. Their faith will be steady and strong because they are familiar with the truth. The truth that they learn as children will carry them for the rest of their days.

As a grandmother you have the privilege of discipling your grandchildren without the pressure and stress of daily parenting. You can give your grandchildren a great gift by teaching them who God is. Your mind isn't filled with school schedules, appointments, or how to deal with the latest squabble. You can teach them about who God is from a place of wisdom, humility, and calmness.

Father, help me take every opportunity to share how magnificent you are with my grandkids!

PERSEVERE AND WIN

Blessed is the one who perseveres under trial because, having stood the test, that person will receive the crown of life that the Lord has promised to those who love him.

JAMES 1:12 NIV

No matter how many years stand between us and our parenting days, we all remember times of frustration. We all had days when we didn't think we could possibly carry on. We doubted our abilities as mothers and wondered if we were ruining everything. We carried the heavy weight of our inadequacy and ideally learned how to surrender it to the Lord.

Have you shared that with your kids? When they feel insecure about their own parenting, it might help to know that they aren't alone. It can encourage them to know that you stayed the course even during your toughest days. Tell your children about how God was faithful to you. Remind them that if he helped you, he will also help them. You are a walking, breathing testimony of perseverance. Let your children see all the ways that you endured!

Father, remind me of all the ways you carried me through parenting. Teach me how to share your faithfulness with my children.

LEARN FROM OTHERS

When we get together, I want to encourage you in your faith, but I also want to be encouraged by yours.

ROMANS 1:12 NLT

As grandparents we bear the privilege that experience and age bring. We've been through a lot and have the battle scars to prove it. It can be tempting to think that it's our job to pass all our life lessons on to our children and grandchildren.

Though you have so much to give your children and grandchildren, remember that you can receive from them as well. You can learn from the way that they seek the Lord and from the ways that they honor him. Their choices may be different from yours but by God's grace, they will live a life that pleases him. You can support and honor your family by having the humility to be encouraged by the unique creation that they are.

Father, help me to learn from my children and grandchildren. I know that you are doing beautiful things in each of their lives.

THE GOOD NEWS

I am not ashamed of the gospel, for it is the power of God that brings salvation to everyone who believes, to the Jew first and also to the Greek.

ROMANS 1:16 ESV

The way we choose to love Jesus can have a lifelong impact on our grandchildren. We might have stories of regret and shame or of triumph and joy. Either way, God is honored when we give him the glory for carrying us through your days. No matter what our testimony sounds like, God can use it in the lives of our grandchildren.

Your testimony can leave a lasting mark on each of their lives. God has led you through each of your days with kindness and grace. There are countless ways that he has shown up for you. You now have the great and wonderful task of sharing that with the children in your life. Tell them unashamedly what he has done for you! Don't be afraid to share how the gospel has personally impacted you.

Father, help me share your faithfulness with my grandchildren. I want to boldly share all that you have done for me.

FOLLOW GOD'S WILL

Ruth replied, "Don't urge me to leave you or to turn back from you. Where you go I will go, and where you stay I will stay. Your people will be my people and your God my God."

RUTH 1:16 NIV

We hope that our children and grandchildren will always live nearby so we can be part of their daily lives. We would love to be there for the milestones and the mundane. The reality is that we cannot control where our children choose to put down roots. As much as we wish they were close, it's important to let them follow God's leading in their lives.

When you encourage your children to follow God's leading remember that he may lead them further away from you. You can still love your grandchildren in a beautiful way, even if they aren't in the same town as you. They are safe in God's hands, and he will be faithful to lead them well. Encourage them to follow him, no matter where he asks them to go.

Father, no matter where my children land, help them to honor you. Teach me how to encourage them even when I am missing them.

WONDERFULLY CREATED

Since the world was created, people have seen the earth and sky. Through everything God made, they can clearly see his invisible qualities—his eternal power and divine nature. So they have no excuse for not knowing God.

ROMANS 1:20 NLT

God's handiwork is everywhere. From the blue sky to the majestic mountains, we are reminded of the divine Creator. In the same way, grandchildren are the work of his hands. Their lives are a reminder that God is a faithful and kind creator. He knit each of them together and loves them dearly.

Each of your grandchildren is a gift. They reflect God and should stir up thanksgiving in your heart. Just like a beautiful sunset causes you to marvel at God's creativity, so can the lives of your grandchildren. They are a miracle, a delight, and a masterpiece made by God.

Father, thank you for the beauty of your creation. Help me to remember that each of my grandchildren is a gift from you.

STAY FOCUSED

We must pay the most careful attention, therefore, to what we have heard, so that we do not drift away.

HEBREWS 2:1 NIV

We've all tried to read a book to a child with a short attention span. A couple of pages are read and it's time for the next favorite book, and then the next, and then the next. This might seem like silly, childish behavior but it's something adults engage in as well. We forget what is truly important and are easily distracted by our own thoughts and ideas.

Following God takes diligence and consistency. The more you pay attention to Scripture, the more it will impact your life. When you find yourself getting distracted from what Scripture says, turn to the Lord and ask him for help. He will faithfully keep you on the narrow path as you follow him.

Father, help me to consistently read your Word. I want to stay focused on what you say so that I can teach my grandchildren about who you are.

MINE!

Let each of you look out not only for his own interests,
but also for the interests of others.

Philippians 2:4 NKJV

Children aren't the only ones who have a hard time sharing. Even as grandparents, we like our stuff. Whether it's belongings, time, or service, it can be tempting to have a tight grasp on what is ours. God wants us to help others, give freely, and to walk with humility. We must, as God's children, loosen our grasp on material things, schedules, and interests.

As a grandparent, you can exercise daily the muscle of generosity. Give unconditionally to your grandchildren. Don't just think about what you want your grandparenting experience to be. Instead, think about what their needs, or your children's needs might be. No matter your age, you can love well and prioritize the interests of others.

Jesus, give me a heart like yours so I can learn to love others as you do. I want to be selfless with all that you've given me.

SEEK RIGHTLY

For those who are self-seeking and do not obey the truth, but obey unrighteousness, there will be wrath and fury.

ROMANS 2:8 ESV

Having lived a life serving God, we know the weight this scripture bears. We know the desperation for our loved ones to follow Jesus and be counted as obedient. We've spent countless minutes praying for our own children and now do the same for our grandchildren. Our highest hope is that our grandchildren would not be self-seeking but that they would seek the Lord.

Pray that your grandchildren will grow in wisdom, humility, and favor with God. Intercede that they would surrender their lives to the Savior and serve him faithfully. Ask God to give them undivided hearts so that they can love and obey him for all their days.

Father, please give my adult children wisdom to raise their children in a way that honors you and equips them to follow you well.

PRECIOUS HANDIWORK

We are God's handiwork, created in Christ Jesus to do good works, which God prepared in advance for us to do.

Ephesians 2:10 NIV

Joy, hope, and expectation fill our hearts at the sight of a newborn grandchild. We marvel at the little person God has created, and they immediately capture our deepest affections. Everything about them is perfect and good. It's a wonderful privilege to be able to watch our children become parents.

Rejoice and praise the Lord for your grandchildren! He has already counted their days, planned good works for them, and knows how their life will be played out. They are his handiwork, and he delights in them. As they grow, remind them of who they are. Let truth be interwoven into your conversations and let your actions toward them reflect who God is.

Father, help me to teach my grandkids the truth about who they are. I know that you have good things in store for them.

FOLLOW OBEDIENTLY

"May the LORD repay you for what you have done. May you be richly rewarded by the LORD, the God of Israel, under whose wings you have come to take refuge."

RUTH 2:12 NIV

As believers, we commit to following Jesus wherever he may lead us. We may be called to leave our homes and move far away from family. God asks us to surrender to him and trust that he holds all our days in his hands. If we hold rigidly to our own plans, we will undoubtedly miss God's blessings and rewards.

If God has you in a season of living far from your children and grandchildren, trust that he knows what he is doing. Just like Ruth, you might be asked to leave your homeland and follow God's leading. Ruth trusted God and found the redemption she needed. The sacrifice feels great, but you will surely find a rich reward in Christ. He will be faithful to order your steps and lead you well.

Father, teach me to submit to your will without conditions.

PRIORITIZE THE WORD

Do your best to present yourself to God as one approved, a worker who has no need to be ashamed, rightly handling the word of truth.

2 Timothy 2:15 ESV

We are living in times when biblical truth is often distorted and taken out of context. More than ever, we need to be familiar with the Word. If God's Word is deeply rooted in our hearts, then we won't be deceived by the lies of the world. We will stand firm and unwavering. Anxiety will take a back seat and no matter how tumultuous things seem, we will trust in what we know is true.

As you walk in the truth, undoubtedly your grandchildren will reap the benefits. As you trust in God, your family will see what it looks like to live a life that honors him. Your days are no longer filled with crying babies, dirty diapers, and the unending needs of your small children. Read the Word and spend time in prayer. Your faithfulness in doing so can impact your entire family.

Father, help me study Scripture well. I want to be able to decipher what is true in all circumstances.

IN YOUR HEART

Mary kept all these things in her heart
and thought about them often.

Luke 2:19 NLT

Our entire lives are made up of divine encounters. God is continuously at work whether we notice or not. Mary is wonderful example of being spiritually receptive to what God is doing. She watched Jesus' life unfold in front of her and she peacefully took in every aspect of it. She probably didn't have a full revelation of what his life would look like, but she trusted that God was at work. When we practice the art of quiet obedience, we learn to trust God more than man.

During the grandparenting years of your life you have the privilege of sharing all your divine encounters with your grandchildren. You have stored up countless memories of what God has done, and you can testify to his great faithfulness. Like Mary, you have a treasure trove of truth inside your heart. Ask God how you can share those treasures with the ones you love.

Father, I treasure the way that you have faithfully led me. Teach me how to share all that you've done for me.

TURN FROM SIN

LORD, you must hear my prayer,
for you are faithful to your promises.
Answer my cry, O righteous God!

PSALM 143:1 TPT

David, the author of this psalm, was vividly aware of his own sins and the need to seek God's forgiveness. He asked God to notice him and hear his prayer. He had experienced God's grace before, and he trusted that when he confessed his sins, God would forgive them. It is important that our grandchildren understand God's mercy and grace. Every act of disobedience is an opportunity to teach them how to repent and seek forgiveness.

Alongside your children, you can help your grandchildren understand what it means to turn from sin. You can encourage them to confess and trust that God will give them a fresh start. Furthermore, you can demonstrate what it looks like to live humbly before God. Your own quick repentance is the best teacher.

Jesus, thank you for your forgiveness. Help me to be quick to repent so that I can demonstrate what it looks like to lean on you for redemption.

ALL THROUGH CHRIST

It is not that we think we are qualified to do anything on our own. Our qualification comes from God.

2 Corinthians 3:5 NLT

Even on our best days, we don't come close to meeting God's standard of perfection. Only through Christ's sacrifice can we stand rightly before God. This is the basic truth of the gospel.

We can try to do everything on our own or we can access the insights and capabilities of the Creator of the universe.

Let this way of living define you as a grandparent. Embrace your weakness, knowing full well that you need new mercy each day. Every day you can call upon the Lord and ask him to help you love your family well. Pray for his anointing, the filling of the Holy Spirit, and the faith to believe you can do all things through Christ.

Father, thank you for giving me all that I need. Help me to rely on your strength over my own. I know my qualification comes from you alone.

RIGHT PRIORITIES

I consider everything a loss because of the surpassing worth of knowing Christ Jesus my Lord, for whose sake I have lost all things. I consider them garbage, that I may gain Christ.

PHILIPPIANS 3:8 NIV

We all have high hopes for our children and grandchildren. We would love to see them flourish in all the ways that life has to offer. It's not wrong to want success, happiness, and satisfaction for your family. However, we need to make sure that we are correctly prioritizing our hopes and dreams. More than anything else, our desire should be for our children and grandchildren to seek Christ.

When it comes to your grandchildren, what do you pray for? Are the requests you bring to God aligned with his Word? Consider the direction of your prayers. Pray that God allows whatever it takes for your loved ones to know him intimately and completely. Pray that they will stand for him, rejoice always, pray consistently, and give thanks in all circumstances.

Father, I pray for my grandbabies to grow in faith. More than anything else, I want them to know you.

CHARACTER FIRST

Put on then, as God's chosen ones, holy and beloved, compassionate hearts, kindness, humility, meekness, and patience.

COLOSSIANS 3:12 ESV

It's easy to get caught up in what we think life should look like while ignoring what really matters. This can happen with our grandchildren as well. We often focus on what kids are doing and accomplishing. Are they doing well in school? Are they prepared for the future? Remember that their character and the state of their heart is more important than any of that.

As a grandparent you can speak into their lives in a unique way. You know full well that life doesn't always turn out the way you think it will but what really matters is to live in a way that honors the Lord. Show them a life lived for Christ, filled with the Holy Spirit, and embracing what really matters.

Father, help my grandchildren to develop godly character. Teach me how to be a good example for them.

ABUNDANT GRACE

I do not mean that I am already as God wants me to be. I have not yet reached that goal, but I continue trying to reach it and to make it mine.

PHILIPPIANS 3:12 NCV

As we get older, we have some distinct choices to make about what kind of person we will be. Our life experience can cause us to walk in bitterness and rigidity or it can cause us to grow in understanding and humility. We get to decide if we will lead our family in a way that encourages them to grow in Christ or shames them for not quite hitting the mark.

Each of your grandchildren is a work in progress. Trust that God is faithfully working in them. Remember the abundant grace that you have been given over the years and extend some of that to your grandkids. When it seems like they are on the wrong path, pray, speak truth, and trust God's leading. He will not abandon them in their wrongdoing, just like he has not abandoned you.

Father, help me to view my grandchildren through your merciful eyes. I trust that you are leading them well.

LOVING DISCIPLINE

The LORD disciplines the ones he loves,
just as a father disciplines the son in whom he delights.

PROVERBS 3:12 CSB

As grandparents, we've all had experience with discipline. When raising our own children, sometimes we got it right and sometimes we didn't. We know how hard it is to stay consistent and soft-hearted at the same time. As we watch our children parent, we can come alongside them and support them as they do their best to raise their kids in a God honoring way.

When you see your child struggling to parent, pray for them. There will be times God might tell you to get involved and there will be times for you to stay out of it. In both circumstances you can practice humility and remember how challenging parenting can be. When help is wanted, approach each situation with gentleness, knowing that it is a privilege to be involved in the lives of others. When help isn't wanted, remember that your prayers and encouraging words are powerful and poignant.

Father, help me to support my children as they learn how to be parents who discipline well. Give me wisdom and discernment.

NEVER PERFECT

Encourage one another daily, as long as it is called "Today," so that none of you may be hardened by sin's deceitfulness.

HEBREWS 3:13 NIV

For as long as we are on this earth, we will continue to sin. The goal for those of us who are Christians is to have a soft heart and a conscience that is sensitive to sin. If we remain humble and teachable, we will not be deceived by sin. We will continually repent and trust in Christ's sacrifice for our salvation. On the other hand, if we refuse to acknowledge our sin, we will get lost in pride and self-sufficiency.

As a grandmother, you can display how to walk in humility. Your grandchildren will see you continuously relying on Christ's sanctification in your life. You can't show them a picture of a finished product or a perfect Christian, but you can be an example of how to stay soft hearted and open to correction. You can encourage them daily and help them to trust in Jesus.

Father, keep my heart devoted to you. Help me to humbly bring my sin to you without delay.

TEACH DILIGENTLY

All Scripture is inspired by God and is useful for teaching, for showing people what is wrong in their lives, for correcting faults, and for teaching how to live right.

2 TIMOTHY 3:16 NCV

We all want to see our grandchildren live in a way that honors God. We want them to seek him daily and trust in his Word. Depending on where they spend most of their time, they may or may not receive consistent biblical teaching. As grandparents, we can support our children by providing help in this area. We can create an atmosphere of openness, in which our grandchildren feel comfortable asking questions and digging into their faith.

If you want to see your grandchildren prioritize the truth of scripture, you'll have to first prioritize it in your own life. Read the Word daily. Ask God to soften your heart and approach his Word with humility. Share what you are learning with your grandchildren. Your family will be encouraged by the way that you approach the Word with teachability.

Father, write your Word on my heart. As I learn more about you, help me to teach my grandchildren.

FEBRUARY

Grandchildren are the crown of the aged,
and the glory of children is their fathers.

PROVERBS 17:6 ESV

UNTO THE LORD

Whatever you do, in word or deed, do everything in the name of the Lord Jesus, giving thanks to God the Father through him.

COLOSSIANS 3:17 ESV

We often dedicate our jobs or ministries to the Lord, asking him to help us succeed. We ask for his help because we know he cares about each detail of our lives. Remember that we can do the same within our families. God wants to see our relationships with our children and grandchildren succeed. He wants to see families operate in a healthy way.

Just as you sought to parent in a way that honored God, you can seek to grandparent in a way that honors him. As you interact with your grandchildren, do it in the name of the Lord. Let your words and actions toward them reflect who God is. Let the way you love your grandchildren be an act of worship. Keep your heart soft toward God's leading and love your family the way that Christ loves them.

Father, show me how to honor you in everything I do and say. Help me to reflect you well.

WORD AND DEED

We should love people not only with words and talk, but by our actions and true caring.

1 John 3:18 NCV

It's not uncommon for someone to say they will do something but then drop the ball. People's words don't always line up with their actions. We are called to believe what is true but to also follow up with legitimate actions. Our faith is meaningless if it doesn't impact the way that we behave. We can't just say that we follow Jesus but refuse to change anything in our life. In the same way, we cannot simply say that we are good grandparents but not do anything about it.

If you want to love your grandchildren well, it will take your time, energy, and resources. If you want to disciple them in the Word, it will take effort and intention. If you want to support your children as parents, it will take time and patience. You get to decide what type of grandparent you will be and then follow up that choice with action.

Father, help me to be the kind of grandparent you want me to be. Help me to love my family in word and deed.

ALWAYS OBEDIENT

"Those whom I love I rebuke and discipline.
So be earnest and repent."

REVELATION 3:19 NIV

As grandparents, we are of an age where we have hopefully lived and learned. We know that it is better to obey directions the first time than to suffer the consequences of needing to correct things later. However, experience doesn't make us impermeable to sin. Each day we must choose to walk humbly before God, opening ourselves up to his correction and discipline. We must let the Holy Spirit search our hearts and show us areas that need repentance and forgiveness.

As you are diligent in your own awareness of sin, you can teach your grandchildren to do the same. Encourage your grandchildren to obey the initial time they are asked. Tell them how it pleases not only their earthly parents, but most importantly their heavenly Father. Explain the peace that comes from living within God's favor. Acknowledge their obedience and let them know God is pleased with them.

Father, help me exhibit obedience to my loved ones. Keep my heart soft and help me to be a good example for my family.

EARTHLY VS ETERNAL

We are citizens of heaven, where the Lord Jesus Christ lives. And we are eagerly waiting for him to return as our Savior.

PHILIPPIANS 3:20 NLT

As we walk in this weary world, what a joy it is to reflect on and anticipate our heavenly home. When we live as citizens of heaven, it fills our hearts with hope for the future. We know and rejoice that the lover of our souls, our bridegroom, has gone ahead and prepared a place for us. This knowledge inspires us to run our race well as we remember that Jesus waits for us at the end.

Remind your family of this great hope. Help them to decipher between what is earthly and what is eternal. Pray that your grandchildren will grow up in a home that has eternity in its sights. Having more experience means that you can share with them how fleeting life is and how to stay focused on what really matters.

Father, fill me with the hope of Christ's return. Help me to teach my family how to focus on what is eternal.

CONSTANT NEED

"I stand at the door and knock. If you hear my voice and open the door, I will come in, and we will share a meal together as friends."

REVELATION 3:20 NLT

As humans, we tend to see things in terms of being completed or unfinished. We like timelines to be linear and for steps to be logical. We want to learn something, and then be done with it. While some things work well with this mindset, our relationship with God does not. Fellowship with Jesus is continuous and unending. There will never be a point in any of our lives when we are done seeking the Lord. Our need for him doesn't change and his desire to be with us certainly doesn't waver.

Jesus is always near, always available, and always ready for communion. Your need for Jesus won't lessen and he won't ever *move on* to someone who needs him more. You are just as valuable to him as the day that you first turned his way. You matter immensely to him, and he is ready and waiting for you to seek him out.

Jesus, help me to seek you all my days. Don't let my age keep me from understanding my need for you.

MADE PERFECT

He will take our weak mortal bodies and change them into glorious bodies like his own, using the same power with which he will bring everything under his control.

PHILIPPIANS 3:21 NLT

As grandparents, we are perfectly aware of our age. Our spirit might feel young, but our bodies show the wear and tear of a life well lived. Whether we are dealing with an unexpected illness or the expected aches and pains that come with age, we know that our bodies aren't as vibrant as they once were.

Maybe keeping up with the grandkids is a struggle or maybe you feel discouraged that you can't do what you once could. No matter the situation, remember that a new day is coming. There will be a time when all things will be made new. Jesus will come back and make the wrong things right; this includes you and your body! You will be made perfect, not lacking anything. When he returns, you will be changed in a moment and all your aches and pains will be forgotten.

Jesus, help me to remember that one day you will make all things new.

NO SECOND CHANCES

Since the promise of entering his rest still stands, let us be careful that none of you be found to have fallen short of it.

HEBREWS 4:1 NIV

When judgment day arrives, those who trust in Christ will receive the promise of his eternal presence and love. Those who have refused the way of salvation will not receive a second chance. Today, is full of new mercies. God is patient and desires that all would know him and be saved.

As you watch your family grow, so does the desire for each of them to know the Lord personally. You want each new member of your family to seek salvation and find redemption in the cross. Continue to pray for them and trust that God will be faithful to meet them at the right time.

God, I desperately want each of my children and grandchildren to know you. Move in their lives and draw them closer to you.

TRULY SATISFIED

Your unfailing love is better than life itself;
how I praise you!

Psalm 63:3 NLT

We often long for what we don't have but once we get it, are less satisfied than we'd hoped. Nothing we work toward, buy, or achieve in this life can truly satisfy our deepest longings. Nothing answers that yearning except Jesus. We can dream, scheme, and work to have it all, but nothing can ever come close to what Christ has to offer.

Through Jesus, you are forgiven and chosen. His love will bring you more satisfaction than any picture-perfect version of your life. If you are feeling dissatisfied, ask the Holy Spirit to reveal why. He will help you evaluate your life from God's perspective and show you areas where you need Christ's love to transform you.

Jesus, you are all I want or need. Help me to find great satisfaction in you.

THANKFULNESS

Rejoice in the Lord always.
Again I will say, rejoice!

Philippians 4:4 NKJV

We all agree that it's good to be thankful, but do we ever truly engage in continuous rejoicing? God deserves our praise, even during hardships. Think of all he has done for us. Recall his faithful provision and deliverance. Engaging in thanksgiving can take us from disappointment to peace and contentedness.

You get to decide what kind of person you want to be. You can walk through your later years with grace and thanksgiving, or you can get lost in disappointment. Reflect and consider how your loved ones see you. Will they remember that Grandma glorified the name of God, or will they remember a negative attitude? As you live a life full of rejoicing, your loved ones will follow suit.

Father, help me live with continual gratitude for your blessings and faithfulness!

GOOD THOUGHTS

Whatever is true, whatever is noble, whatever is right,
whatever is pure, whatever is lovely, whatever is admirable—
if anything is excellent or praiseworthy—
think about such things.

PHILIPPIANS 4:8 NIV

Our thoughts are more powerful than we realize. We base our actions, consciously or subconsciously, on what fills our minds. This is why it's so important to be aware of what we dwell on. If we ascribe to negativity, it will spill out into our lives. If we fill our minds with what is good and true, our actions will follow.

If you have noticed some patterns in your life that you aren't happy with, consider the state of your mind. Ask the Holy Spirit for help and adopt a new way of thinking. Memorize Scripture, count your blessings, sing worship songs, and remember to see yourself as God sees you. As your thoughts change, so will your patterns, actions, and habits.

Father, help me to think in a way that honors you. Help me to focus on what is good and right.

WHAT MATTERS

We toil and strive, because we have our hope set on the living God, who is the Savior of all people, especially of those who believe.

1 TIMOTHY 4:10 ESV

This portion of Timothy reminds readers not to get caught in rules or expectations that don't really matter. We aren't supposed to be derailed by people who eat a certain way or declare their opinions as the highest authority. Instead, we are called to live in a way that honors God and the sacrifice that Jesus made.

In the later years of your life, you may have found that your habits look different than they did when you were young. Ideally, your faith is stronger now than it was then. You aren't easily swayed by the opinions of others, and you know what really matters. If you don't feel secure in this way, ask the Holy Spirit for help. He will give you discernment and teach you how to live.

Help me fulfill your will, Lord. I want to strive only for what pleases you.

CHRIST IN US

Unless the LORD builds the house,
the builders labor in vain.
Unless the LORD watches over the city,
the guards stand watch in vain.

PSALM 127:1 NIV

If success is what we are after, we must walk in the favor of the Lord. There is nothing we can do on our own that would not be better if done in God's way. After all, he is the author and perfector of everything. His ways are always better than ours. If we strive to accomplish things alone, we will miss the mark.

This can be applied to the way you approach grandparenting. You can seek to love your family in our own strength, or you can submit your relationships to God and do things in his way. This means being open to correction and trusting the Holy Spirit for guidance in what you say and how you act. When you let God define what it means to be a good grandparent, you can have confidence that he will lead you rightly.

Father, thank you for being steady and reliable. I want to do things your way.

LIFELONG STUDENT

The word of God is alive and active. Sharper than any double-edged sword, it penetrates even to dividing soul and spirit, joints and marrow; it judges the thoughts and attitudes of the heart.

HEBREWS 4:12 NIV

God's Word can challenge, reveal, and correct what's hidden in our heart. It has the power to convict, teach, guide, and encourage. There is no need to worry or walk in confusion when we have unlimited access to the wisdom of God. When we devote time to the study of Scripture, we equip ourselves to stay on the narrow path.

Teach your grandchildren the value of hiding truth in their hearts. Lead by example when it comes to memorizing Scripture. Pray truth over them and show them what it looks like to be a lifelong student of scripture. Show them how the Bible is a good gift and not intimidating or difficult to understand. Show them your love and reverence for the Bible and ask the Holy Spirit to give them a love for scripture as well.

Father, help me crave your Word, desiring it more each day.

SACRIFICIAL LOVE

"He will renew your life and sustain you in your old age. For your daughter-in-law, who loves you and who is better to you than seven sons, has given him birth."

RUTH 4:15 NIV

Naomi found herself in a desperate situation as a widow with no living sons. She gave her daughters in law the opportunity to leave and find husbands, but Ruth was faithful to Naomi. She stayed by her side and trusted that God would provide for them both.

As the matriarch of your family, you can embody this type of self-sacrificial affection. You can be the first one to lay down your agenda and love your family in a way that pleases God. Set aside your own desires and ask God to teach you how put the desires of others first. This might mean giving up your time, energy, or ideas of what grandparenting should look like. God does amazing things when we offer our lives unselfishly.

Father, help me love unselfishly and in a way that puts others first.

NOTHING IS HIDDEN

Nothing in all creation is hidden from God's sight. Everything is uncovered and laid bare before the eyes of him to whom we must give account.

HEBREWS 4:13 NIV

No matter how tricky or cunning we think we are, we cannot hide anything from God. He knows the deepest recesses of our hearts and he sees our intentions clearly. We cannot fool him or expect him to forget anything. When we think of God in this way, we might feel intimidated or ashamed of our own sin. Instead, we should let God's ability to see everything bring us great comfort.

It would make sense to be nervous before God if he were hateful, harsh, or unloving. But he is none of those things. God is eternally kind, always loving, and gentle beyond understanding. You don't ever have to be nervous or afraid of his ability to see you clearly. Because of Jesus, you are seen through eyes of mercy and belonging.

Father, help me to quickly seek forgiveness when I sin.

NUMBER YOUR DAYS

Teach us to number our days carefully
so that we may develop wisdom in our hearts.

Psalm 90:12 CSB

As young women we see our lives laid before us, expansive and full of promise. We see endless opportunity and no end in sight when it comes to accomplishing our dreams. As we get older, we realize how fleeting life is. We know how valuable our time is and in our later years might really begin to question what we do with it.

As a grandmother, new or seasoned, you might be keenly aware that your days are numbered. Your youth is behind you, and you might be unsure of what the future will look like. Don't let this realization discourage you. Instead, commit each day to the Lord. Trust in his leadership. He knows exactly what your life will look like, both as a young woman and as someone with a few more gray hairs. He does not fret or worry, and neither should you.

Father, help me number my days and surrender them to you.

ALL THINGS

I can do all things through Christ,
because he gives me strength.

PHILIPPIANS 4:13 NCV

In Philippians, Paul talks about living in seasons of plenty and in seasons of wanting. He describes how sometimes his life has been overflowing with abundant goodness and sometimes it has been incredibly difficult. When he says he can do all things through Christ, what he means is that in any circumstance, he can follow Jesus and find satisfaction in him. This verse has more to do with the state of our hearts than accomplishing the things we want.

As a grandmother, you can embody this way of living for your family. You, like Paul, have probably walked through many different seasons of life. Seasons where you have had all you need, and seasons of doubt or worry. You can testify to your family that God was present in all of it. He was always with you and was faithful to lead you. No matter what your life has looked like, Christ has never abandoned you.

Father, just as I have before, help me to trust in you no matter what my circumstances are.

ALWAYS UNDERSTANDING

We do not have a high priest who is unable to empathize with our weaknesses, but we have one who has been tempted in every way, just as we are—yet he did not sin.

HEBREWS 4:15 NIV

We have all felt alone in our sorrows. We've all had days when it seemed like no one else could possibly understand our pain. We might be justified in the complexity of what we are going through, but the truth is that we are never alone. Jesus knows the ins and out of everything we experience. He is not far away and disconnected. Instead, he is close and full of understanding.

No matter what you walk through as a grandmother, you have an ally in Jesus. He will always understand what you are going through. He is your advocate and your wise council. You can bring him the most complicated family situation and he can bring clarity and direction.

Jesus, what a comfort to know that you understand all I go through. Thank you for always being nearby.

TRUE CONFIDENCE

Let us then approach God's throne of grace with confidence, so that we may receive mercy and find grace to help us in our time of need.

HEBREWS 4:16 NIV

God invites us to draw close so we can confess our sins and receive the forgiveness we need. We are invited to go boldly into his presence because Christ's sacrifice has paved the way for us. Our confidence doesn't come from drumming up the right feelings but from believing that what Jesus has done on the cross is all that's needed to qualify us.

Teach this truth to your grandchildren. Show them that their good deeds aren't the reason they are accepted and loved. Their acceptance comes from being a child of God. Their behavior isn't what qualifies them to be in God's presence, or yours. Show them that God's mercy and grace far exceeds their own goodness.

Father, thank you for setting the example of how to extend grace and mercy to my grandchildren.

ALL WE NEED

My God will supply all your needs according to his riches in glory in Christ Jesus.

PHILIPPIANS 4:19 NASB

There can be a vast discrepancy in what our needs are. We all have different ideas about what makes a comfortable life. Some count material luxuries as a need, believing that God's good gifts should come with a high price tag. For others, having a roof over their heads and food on the table is satisfactory. No matter what our personal opinions are, God knows exactly what we need. If we align our expectations with his desires, we'll never be left wanting.

As a grandmother, you've lived long enough to have experienced God's provision. He has carried you for all your days and he deserves all the glory. In these later years of your life, remember to acknowledge all that God has done. Thank him for the way that he has provided for you and continue to trust in him for what you need now.

Jesus, thank you for always taking care of me. Help me to trust you for everything I need.

WHAT YOU ALLOW

Above all else, guard your heart,
for everything you do flows from it.

PROVERBS 4:23 NIV

Multiple times in scripture we are warned to pay attention to what we allow into our hearts and minds. The things we think about can impact every other part of our lives. When we fill our hearts with impurity, negativity, and worldly values, we will surely act in those ways. This is why God says to guard our hearts. We should pay attention to what we take in and be diligent in the way we protect ourselves.

These types of commands don't change as you age. Even as a grandmother, it's wise to be aware of the types of things you are consuming on a regular basis. With humility, be aware of how God has asked you to live. Pray that your grandchildren will do the same. Ask God to give them soft hearts and grace to respond rightly to his guidance.

Jesus, help me guard my heart. Give me awareness and discernment about what I watch, listen to, and allow into my life.

EMOTIONAL GROWTH

"In your anger do not sin": Do not let the sun go down while you are still angry.

EPHESIANS 4:26 NIV

We all have different thresholds for anger. Some of us may find our blood boiling when we're cut off in traffic while others may feel enraged by excess noise or the defiance of others. Despite what causes it, our anger is not necessarily the problem. God knows that we will experience anger. What matters most is how we handle it. We are instructed not to sin in our anger.

No matter what pushes your buttons, you are asked to have a controlled response. If you lash out at others, or cause damage to people or property, you have crossed a line. The good news is that no matter what your age, there is room to grow in this area. Ask God how you can better handle your anger. The more you learn to manage your emotions in a healthy way, the more you can lead your family in the same practice.

Father, help me to be aware of my own unhealthy reactions. Teach me how to honor you when my feelings are overwhelming.

ENCOURAGE OTHERS

Do not let any unwholesome talk come out of your mouths, but only what is helpful for building others up according to their needs, that it may benefit those who listen.

EPHESIANS 4:29 NIV

We all probably have different definitions of unwholesome talk. We could argue and point fingers, or we can focus on the way that Ephesians tells us to speak. The clear and defining factor for speech that pleases God is that it builds up others. Instead of trying to make a list of what's allowed and what isn't, instead remember that first and foremost we are asked to encourage those around us.

As a grandmother, your words matter. Your grandchildren won't be impacted by the rules that you told them to follow. They will be impacted by the way that your words made them feel. Do you encourage, lift up, and exhort them? Prioritize encouraging your grandchildren over voicing disapproval or frustration.

God, please help me to guard my tongue. I want my words to point my grandchildren to you.

QUICK TO FORGIVE

Be kind and compassionate to one another,
forgiving each other, just as in Christ God forgave you.

EPHESIANS 4:32 NIV

Especially in our relationships, we are bound to make a lot of mistakes. There are plenty of times when we say or do the wrong thing and hurt someone's feelings. We get caught up in our own concerns and forget to think about the needs of others. We hope that the people who love us will be forgiving even when we make mistakes. If that's our hope, then we should treat others in the same way.

Be forgiving of little grievances. Don't let offense pile up in your heart. Your children or grandchildren may let you down or cause frustration, but God's command is that you forgive quickly, just as he has forgiven you. As you practice extending forgiveness, your life will be filled with more joy and less stress.

Jesus, help me to forgive quickly and love as you do.

GOOD GIFTS

He fills my life with good things.
My youth is renewed like the eagle's!

PSALM 103:5 NLT

We all love giving our grandchildren gifts. Seeing the excitement on their little faces is an amazing reward. It's fun to be able to bless them and add joy to their lives. This gift-giving desire is from our heavenly Father. He loves to give good gifts to his children. He is generous, kind, and knows exactly what we need.

How can you practice being a good gift giver with your grandchildren? You don't need an endless bank account to make them feel loved and noticed. You could send them little cards or bless them with baked goods. You can give the gift of time and experience. There are hundreds of ways that you can cultivate generosity in your life. In doing so, you reflect the character of God.

God, I want to be thoughtful and generous like you. Show me how I can bless my grandchildren.

CONTINUE TO PRAY

The widow who is really in need and left all alone puts her hope in God and continues night and day to pray and to ask God for help.

1 TIMOTHY 5:5 NIV

There aren't any life circumstances that separate us from God. Even a widow, whose days are lonely, can put her hope in God. None of us look forward to that potential season of life but it's important to recognize that even in loss and loneliness, we are asked to depend on the Lord. Especially in our grief, God is near. Even when we walk through something as horrible as saying goodbye to a spouse, we are supposed to continuously ask God for help.

If this is the season you are in, lean on the one who created you and knows you inside and out. God sees the complexity of your emotions and the pain of being alone. He will never forsake you, especially in your grief. Ask him for help and let him lead you.

Father, help me navigate this unknown season. I want to lean on you.

ALL HOPE

This hope will not lead to disappointment. For we know how dearly God loves us, because he has given us the Holy Spirit to fill our hearts with his love.

ROMANS 5:5 NLT

We've all experienced some doubt in our walk with the Lord. Whether we question the strength of our own faith or get stumped by something in scripture, doubt or disbelief is not abnormal. Issues arise when our doubts push us further away from God instead of toward him. Remember that we have the Holy Spirit to fill our hearts with love and teach us what is true.

As a grandmother, you can use your seasons of doubt to encourage your grandchildren. They may look at your age and assume that you've had a clear, unobstructed walk with the Lord. You can show them the reality of what a faith-filled life looks like. Knowing that you had times of disappointment and disbelief can encourage them to persevere when they face their own obstacles.

Father, thank you for always carrying me through doubt. Continue to give me hope and help me to encourage my grandchildren.

GREAT SACRIFICE

God demonstrates his own love for us in this:
While we were still sinners, Christ died for us.

ROMANS 5:8 NIV

Our worst mess is not too much for God. He is not intimidated by our mistakes or turned off by our shortcomings. In fact, our worst brings out his best. When we were completely lost in sin, Christ died for us. He did not wait until we cleaned ourselves up. He did not stand, arms crossed and finger pointing, telling us to get our act together. Jesus knew how undeserving we all are and yet he willingly sacrificed everything.

If you want to love your grandchildren well, look to Jesus as an example. Look at how Jesus treats your sins and your weaknesses. He does not approach you harshly with a list of rules and expectations. He approaches you with kindness and great sacrifice. Let this be the foundation for the way that you love your family.

Jesus, thank you for your sacrifice which saved me. Help me to love my family the way you love me.

MARCH

I am reminded of your sincere faith,
a faith that first dwelt in your
grandmother Lois and your
mother Eunice and now,
I am sure, dwells in you as well.

2 TIMOTHY 1:5 ESV

PRAISE ALWAYS

From the rising of the sun to its going down
the LORD's name is to be praised.

PSALM 113:3 NKJV

So often we hear believers asking for prayer so they can discern and learn God's will. While this is a good thing to do, sometimes we overlook that he has already shared his will with us in clear ways. Scripture tells us that we are to praise the Lord from the time we wake up to the time we lay our heads down. He is worthy of our praise from morning to night.

This is something that you can embody and display for your grandchildren. Young believers often struggle with the concept of God's will. They want to accomplish great things and have clear direction. You can be a steady pillar of faith, reminding them that the everyday posture of their heart is far more important than grandiose plans for pleasing God. As you live a life filled with praise, your grandchildren will see what it looks like to honor God.

Father, help me to know and obey your Word. Help me teach my grandchildren how to live a life of praise.

SHARE IN SUFFERING

The God of all grace, who called you to his eternal glory in Christ, after you have suffered a little while, will himself restore you and make you strong, firm and steadfast.

1 PETER 5:10 NIV

What a promise this verse holds! We are reminded that we will one day stand in the presence of God. Until that wonderful day, 1 Peter reminds us that God is merciful and that he will walk with us through whatever we encounter. We are assured that we will suffer for only a short time. Soon the pain we have endured will be over and we will be looking into the eyes of Jesus in the heavenly home he has prepared for us.

This is your greatest calling, to faithfully endure until you are called home or Christ returns. When you let this calling impact every area of your life, your family will surely take notice. What a blessing it is for your grandchildren to see you walk humbly before God, trusting in his truth, consistently filled with the hope of his return.

Jesus, give me courage to faithfully wait for you. Help me to show my grandchildren what it means to follow you.

WORD AND DEED

I am passionately in love with God because he listens to me. He hears my prayers and answers them.

Psalm 116:1 TPT

In this Psalm we learn about two aspects of who God is. First, he listens to us. He hears our cries and notices when we speak. He is not a faraway God who ignores his children. Second, he responds to what we say. He doesn't just listen; he goes a step further and acts. This is the type of love that is displayed for us. We serve a God who hears and responds.

You can love your grandchildren in the same way. It is loving to be aware of them and available to them. You can offer a listening ear and pay attention to what is important to them. Furthermore, you can love them by responding to what they say and do. Follow up on promises that you make and show up when it counts. When you love in both word and deed, you love in the same way that God loves.

Jesus, help me love my grandchildren in the same way that you love me.

CLEAR GUIDELINES

Warn those who are lazy. Encourage those who are timid. Take tender care of those who are weak. Be patient with everyone.

1 Thessalonians 5:14 NLT

Sometimes, there is room for interpretation in scripture and sometimes it is incredibly clear. Today's verse is not complicated or difficult to understand. It outlines a clear methodology for how to love well. As we wait for Christ's return, this is how we are supposed to interact with those around us.

If you are ever unsure of how to love your grandchildren, look at this scripture. Be patient always, be tender toward the weak, encourage the timid and warn the lazy. You can probably place each of your grandchildren in one of those categories. Ask God for discernment and then love your family as it is outlined in scripture.

Jesus, help me treat others in the way that scripture outlines. I want to honor you by being obedient to your Word.

LEARN TO DISTINGUISH

Solid food is for the mature, who by constant use have trained themselves to distinguish good from evil.

HEBREWS 5:14 NIV

The more we absorb biblical truth, the more mature we will be in our faith. God's Word brings wisdom and understanding. It allows us to navigate the world rightly and make decisions that honor God. Hebrews says that the mature can distinguish good from evil. This implies that those who are immature cannot always make that distinction. When we don't have a solid foundation of biblical truth, we will be easily swayed by the values of the world.

Depending on the ages or life experience of your grandchildren, you might consider them spiritually immature. You may have noticed them having difficulty deciphering between good and evil. Pray for them! Ask God to give them discernment and to strengthen their faith. Teach them the Word and make yourself available for encouragement and direction when they need it.

Father, help my grandchildren love your Word. Teach them how to navigate the world and decipher between good and evil.

TEACH WELL

Make sure that nobody pays back wrong for wrong, but always strive to do what is good for each other and for everyone else.

1 THESSALONIANS 5:15 NIV

We do not need to teach children to be selfish. The words *mine* and *no* roll off the toddler's tongue like the most natural thing in the world. We are all prone to do what we want and protect what we think is ours. Little acts of defiance are normal for a growing mind. It's our job as parents and grandparents to lovingly correct and teach the little ones in our lives how to express themselves in a healthy way.

As a grandmother you have to opportunity to help teach your grandchildren how to behave in a way that honors God. With their parents' blessing, you can teach them and disciple them. Ask the Holy Spirit to show you opportunities and be faithful to speak the truth in love when the time arises.

Father, help me do good things for other people. Show me how to teach my grandchildren to do the same.

RELY ON TRUTH

I have hidden your word in my heart
that I might not sin against you.

PSALM 119:11 NIV

None of us are without temptation. We each have different sins that we are prone to. We are all faced with decisions between good and evil, enticed by our own sin nature. When temptation arises, we can respond in our own strength, or we can rely on God. We can stand firmly on a foundation of truth and pull from the well of scripture that is hidden in our hearts.

If you have been walking with the Lord for a while, then you have probably exercised the muscle of asking God for help when you are tempted. This might not be the case for your grandchildren. As they grow in their faith, they will not be as familiar with what it takes to stand in truth. When they struggle, strengthen them with the Word. When they fall, encourage them, and remind them that they will get stronger as they store truth in their hearts.

Father, please give my grandchildren a desire to read the Word. Help them to cherish your Word.

GOOD DEEDS

"Let your good deeds shine out for all to see,
so that everyone will praise your heavenly Father."

MATTHEW 5:16 NLT

The older we get the more tempted we might be to check out. We've been through the tumultuous years of figuring out who we are, we've raised our children, and possibly worked in our careers for many years. We might feel tired and weary of doing the right thing. No matter what our flesh says, there isn't a time in life when we get to declare ourselves done. We don't get to check out and stop doing good.

If you feel tired and worn out, ask God to renew your spirit. Scripture is clear that you are to let your good deeds act as a reflection of who God is. The way that you live points to his character and should display his love for all to see. If you are weary of doing that, perhaps you've been operating in your own strength instead of depending on the Holy Spirit to lead you in gentleness and wisdom.

Father, strengthen me from the inside out. I want my good deeds to show the world who you are.

LIFE ISN'T FAIR

"He gives his sunlight to both the evil and the good, and he sends rain on the just and the unjust alike."

MATTHEW 5:45 NLT

As grandparents we have a lot of life experience. We are keenly aware that life is rarely fair. The wicked often win and those with earnest hearts experience pain and suffering. It doesn't always seem right, but we are at least used to it. Our grandchildren haven't had as many opportunities to observe the way the world works. It can be painful to watch them have their eyes opened to injustice and wrongdoing.

As your grandchildren grow and mature, you can be an example of steadfast faith. As their faith is tested by difficult life experiences you can remind them of all that you've been through. You can encourage them that even when things seem unfair, God is in control. You can teach them how to put their faith in what Jesus has done for them and in what he promises to do when he comes back.

Father, help me to have the kind of faith that encourages my grandchildren when they experience wrongdoing.

PATH TO MATURITY

Let us move beyond the elementary teachings about Christ and be taken forward to maturity, not laying again the foundation of repentance from acts that lead to death, and of faith in God.

HEBREWS 6:1 NIV

When we've lived most of our life in devotion to God, we can sometimes forget those early days of stumbling through our beliefs. We weren't always steady and confident. We spent whole seasons absorbing the basic truths of the gospel, letting them sink deep into our hearts. As we matured, we moved beyond those teachings and our faith was strengthened. By God's grace, we developed a relationship with him that is strong, unwavering, and dependent on his strength.

Remember that your faith has been developed over an entire lifetime. Lend the same grace to your family. Be patient when you see your grandchildren struggle. Be diligent in prayer and support their parents with humility, knowing full well that life doesn't always look the way we think it should. Trust that God will lead them, just as he led you, from elementary teachings into the deep waters of a steady faith.

Jesus, lead my grandchildren into maturity. Keep them strong as they learn more about you.

SEEKING APPROVAL

"Be careful! When you do good things, don't do them in front of people to be seen by them. If you do that, you will have no reward from your Father in heaven."

MATTHEW 6:1 NCV

The pharisees made great public gestures in prayer for everyone to see. Their sole motive was to bring attention to themselves. Scripture says when we're seeking approval from men, we lose the reward from our heavenly Father. We need to purify our hearts and do good in the eyes of our heavenly Father alone.

You can take this scripture and apply it to the way that you behave as a grandmother. Are you more concerned with having a picture-perfect family than you are with pleasing the Lord? Do you want those around you to see you being a beloved grandma more than you want to put in the faithful work of leading a family? Ask God to search your heart and reveal any selfish motives to you. He will gently correct you and lead you to repentance.

Father, I only want to glorify you. Keep me from seeking the approval of men.

HEAVENLY REWARDS

"When you pray, don't be like the hypocrites who love to pray publicly on street corners and in the synagogues where everyone can see them. I tell you the truth, that is all the reward they will ever get."

MATTHEW 6:5 NLT

When it comes to our faith, most of what we do won't be seen or noticed by others. What really matters is the state of our hearts and the way we personally interact with the Lord. The same can be said about parenting. Having already raised children, we know that most of the work is thankless. No one notices the steady, behind the scenes work that goes into keeping a family healthy and strong.

This probably hasn't changed as you've become a grandmother. It is still true that your accolades should come from your heavenly father and not from other people. It doesn't matter if other people think you are a good grandmother. All that matters is that you are faithful and obedient to the Lord in this season of your life.

Father, help me to glorify you by being obedient to what you ask of me. I want your rewards, not the accolades of others.

GODLY REQUIREMENTS

What does the LORD require of you?
To act justly and to love mercy
and to walk humbly with your God.

MICAH 6:8 NIV

How many of us agonize over what God's will is for our lives? We ask to hear from him but then we insert our own thoughts, potentially missing altogether what his will might be. We are anxious to avoid missing what God has predestined for us. Instead of agonizing over the unknown we can look to the Word for clear directions about what God wants from us. The requirement is clear: be just in all you do, be merciful to everyone, and have humility.

If you want to honor God with your choices, you can use Scripture as a standard. Ask God to equip you to fulfill what he has commanded. He will be faithful to give you the tools that you need to live a godly life. This was true early on in your life and will be true for all your days.

Thank you, Father, for telling me exactly how to live a life that honors you.

TAKE INVENTORY

Do not let any part of your body become an instrument of evil to serve sin. Instead, give yourselves completely to God, for you were dead, but now you have new life. So use your whole body as an instrument to do what is right for the glory of God.

ROMANS 6:13 NLT

When we were lost, we may have indulged in all types of sinful behavior. However, there is no reason to return to the past and engage in our former ways. We are transformed in Christ, washed in his blood, and empowered by his Spirit. We must commit to living a righteous life, being holy as he is holy.

It's good to take inventory of your spiritual life. What have your eyes been watching? What have your ears been listening to? What guilty pleasures have you given yourself over to? You have the power in Christ to say no to all that would cause you to fall into sin. Recommit yourself daily to living an upright life.

Father, help me make the choices that honor you. I don't want any part of my body to be an instrument for serving sin.

DO GOOD

Tell them to use their money to do good. They should be rich in good works and generous to those in need, always being ready to share with others.

1 Timothy 6:18 NLT

When we've spent our life caring for others it can be tempting to turn down the generosity switch in our hearts. As we get older shouldn't we be able to enjoy all of our hard work splurge a little? We all have different things we daydream about doing with our money. None of them are inherently wrong but are we committed to honoring the Lord with our finances? Scripture tells us to use our money to do good. There is no timeline on this command.

Whether your bank account is flourishing or sparse, God's Word doesn't change. In little and in plenty, you can serve him with your money. You can use what you have to bless others and be generous to those around you. Ask the Holy Spirit to lead you and he will stir your spirit when there is a need you can meet.

Father, thank you for your provision. Help me to be generous with all you have given me.

PRAY ALWAYS

Pray in the Spirit at all times and on every occasion. Stay alert and be persistent in your prayers for all believers everywhere.

EPHESIANS 6:18 NLT

When we pray, we are battling in the spiritual realm. We are engaging with what is unseen and trusting that God hears our cries. When we pray, we are acknowledging the power of God and surrendering control over to him. We pray because we believe that it makes a difference. Even so, certain seasons of life can feel so hectic that we don't engage in prayer nearly enough.

Your grandparenting years are a wonderful time to devote yourself more consistently to prayer. You can be a great blessing to your families by praying for them. Stay engaged in what is going on in their lives and intercede on their behalf. Trust that as you cry out for them, God hears and is moving in their lives.

Holy Spirit, please empower me to pray consistently. Help me to rely on your strength and guidance as I intercede for my family.

FIRM ANCHOR

We have this hope as an anchor for the soul,
firm and secure.

Hebrews 6:19 NIV

We will only experience security and steadfastness when we place our confidence in the Lord. Try as we might, there is no other solution that will truly work. We can battle our fears and anxieties until we are exhausted, but the only reliable anchor we have is the redemption that Jesus brings.

If you find yourself plagued with negative thoughts, lean on the Lord. Ask him to remind you of what is true and good. Ask him to give you a fresh revelation of the gospel. As your mind is renewed by truth, you'll find yourself more at ease in a tumultuous world. From this place of steadfastness, you can lead your family well.

Father, help me to find my security and steadiness in what Christ has done and will do.

COVERED AND SAFE

He will cover you with his feathers,
and under his wings you will find refuge;
his faithfulness will be your shield and rampart.

Psalm 91:4 NIV

Like the warmth and covering of a cozy blanket on a cold winter night, so is the security of the Father's wings in our times of trouble. When trials strike, there is no need to worry about where to go for solace and comfort. We simply cry out to our father, and he protects us. He holds us close as the fierce winds blow. His rampart and shield are likened to a physical barrier to keep evil at bay.

If you are facing hardships, take it to God. Drop your concerns at his feet and trust that he is working on your behalf. Then settle in, get comfortable, and experience the safety of resting in your heavenly Father's arms. Believe that he is in control and is fully capable of handling whatever situation you are in.

Father, thank you for being my comfort and my defender. Teach me how to rest in your presence.

SPEAK TRUTH

The wages of sin is death, but the gift of God is eternal life in Christ Jesus our Lord.

Romans 6:23 NIV

One day our lives will cease, and judgment will come. Christ will defend his own before the heavenly judge, but those who rejected him will have no defense at all. Believers enter their heavenly home while unbelievers are cast out of his presence forever, sentenced to eternal separation from God.

As you look at grandchildren, you probably feel an urgency for their salvation. You want nothing more than for your loved ones than to spend eternity in the presence of God. While you can, speak to them about the truth of God's Word. Pray for them earnestly and ask God to soften their hearts.

Jesus, help me be bold in sharing truth with my family. Show me how to teach my grandchildren about who you are.

MARCH 20

NEW WORRIES

When my anxious thoughts multiply within me,
your comfort delights my soul.

PSALM 94:19 NASB

Anxiety is a constant pest and a waste of precious time. Jesus said that our worries would never accomplish anything. None of us can honestly say that our fretting changed our circumstances or brought about a different outcome. Worrying about something is like living through a worst-case scenario that may never happen. Instead, we are invited to find comfort in the Lord. We can take our thoughts captive and surrender them to Christ.

As you get older your worries may increase. Like with every new season you've walked through, there is no manual for aging. As a grandparent, you'll surely encounter many new experiences. Give your worries to the Lord. Make your requests known to him and then find comfort in his presence.

God, thank you for being a comforting Father. Help me to lean on you when I am worried.

GRATEFULLY CONTENT

"Look at the birds. They don't plant or harvest or store food in barns, for your heavenly Father feeds them. And aren't you far more valuable to him than they are? Can all your worries add a single moment to your life?"

MATTHEW 6:26-27 NLT

God is more aware of our needs than we are. He doesn't turn up his nose to our pleas for help. He hears us and is faithful to provide us with the right things when we ask. How many times do we wonder why we are without something and then realize that we didn't even ask God for help? He loves it when we call on him!

Don't forget to call upon the Lord for what you need. His ear is turned toward you and his infinite resources are available to you. Trust that he sees you and he knows your needs. Society is so focused on satisfaction and personal gain. By trusting in the Lord, your life can be marked by quiet contentedness instead. As you walk in this way, you can be an example to your children and grandchildren of how to have a faith-filled life, trusting that you are taken care of.

Father, thank you for your generous provisions and for knowing exactly what is best for me.

GOOD REST

"Come with me by yourselves to a quiet place and get some rest."

MARK 6:31 NIV

It's common to overcommit your time, energy, and resources. We often want to help as much as we possibly can. The truth is that we all need rest. It is good and right to take a break. When unsure, we can ask the Holy Spirit for discernment. He will always help when our desire is to honor the Lord. If we listen to his voice and are obedient when he says to take a break, we'll find true refreshment.

Maybe you've developed a tendency to overcommit to your grandchildren. You want to be included so you offer to help when you shouldn't. Maybe you're nervous that you'll miss out or that your children will think you don't want to be involved. In this season of life, as tempting as it can be to give without reprieve, remember that rest is good. You were created to need rest. Ask the Holy Spirit to give you discernment when it comes to your commitments.

Father, teach me how to find my rest in you. Help me listen to your voice and take breaks when needed.

ABOVE ALL ELSE

"Seek first the kingdom of God and his righteousness, and all these things shall be added to you."

MATTHEW 6:33 NKJV

Wouldn't it be wonderful if our grandchildren grew up with the knowledge of God and his kingdom more than anything else? There is so much fighting for their attention, but our biggest prayer is that God's voice would be louder than the rest. We hope and pray that even with all the opinions they are faced with, they'll learn to value what God says above all else.

If you are unsure of how to help your grandchildren walk with the Lord, start with prayer. Pray that God would give you opportunities to teach them the truth. Pray that their hearts would be soft and that they would have their eyes opened to who God is. Pray for their protection as they navigate the world and that they will be strong in the face of temptation. As you commit your grandchildren to the Lord, trust that he will be faithful to lead them.

Father, I want my grandchildren to seek you above all else. Help me to teach them who you are.

DON'T WORRY

"Do not worry about tomorrow;
for tomorrow will worry about itself.
Each day has enough trouble of its own."

MATTHEW 6:34 NASB

When we worry, we waste the precious time God has granted us. Instead, we should use it wisely by seeking God, listening for his direction, and doing his will. As our family watches, they will be inspired to do the same. Then, when tomorrow comes, they will face it with the same strength and confidence that we have shown.

If you are in need but you have a heavenly Father who owns the cattle on a thousand hills, why be concerned? Remember all the times that he has been faithful to you in the past. If he has done it once, he will do it again. As the matriarch of your family, you have the unique opportunity to decide if your leadership will be defined by worry or steadfast trust in the one who made you.

Father, help me trust fully in you. I don't want to spend my time worrying.

MIRACLE AFTER MIRACLE

Remember the wondrous works that he has done,
his miracles, and the judgements he uttered.

PSALM 105:5 ESV

God's Word is full of accounts of his miraculous deeds. From the Father's works in the Old Testament to the miracles performed by Jesus in the New Testament, scripture is brimming with his good works. He created the world, breathed life into man, brought about a flood, and parted the Red Sea so his chosen people could escape tyranny. Christ made water into wine, opened the eyes of the blind, and raised a beloved friend from the grave. Miracle after miracle reminds us of how wonderous and faithful God is.

When you are discouraged, remember what God has done in your own life. Just as you can reread biblical accounts of his greatness, you can look back on your own life and recall his good works. What sin has he freed you from? How has he provided for you? How has he sustained your very life? Let his faithfulness stir your heart in affection toward him.

Father, thank you for your miraculous deeds. Help me to remember all that you have done for me.

ASK CONFIDENTLY

"Ask, and the gift is yours. Seek, and you'll discover. Knock, and the door will be opened for you."

MATTHEW 7:7 TPT

Children have no trouble asking for what they want. They are known to even claim something is theirs when it isn't. If only we could have the faith and boldness of a child! We would not hesitate to approach his throne and joyfully ask for what we need. Like a child, we would have absolute assurance that our requests will be granted.

As a grandmother, you're no stranger to the confident and innocent questions of your grandchildren. They ask you for an extra cookie, or a fun toy because they genuinely believe that you might give it to them. In the same way, ask God for what you need! Remember that he loves to give his children good gifts. It brings him joy to be approached by a child who trusts him wholeheartedly.

Thank you, Jesus, for all the good gifts in my life. Help me to ask you for what I need with confidence.

HE LEADS

I just want to obey all you ask of me.
So teach me, Lord, for you are my God.
Your gracious Spirit is all I need,
so lead me on good paths that are pleasing to you,
my one and only God!

Psalm 143:10 TPT

Once we have surrendered our lives to the Savior there is a lifetime of work ahead. We must pay attention to the Holy Spirit's leading so that we stay on the narrow road. The good news is that God is a faithful and wise teacher. We are never alone and are not expected to navigate the Christian life by our own strength. Not only do we get to rely on God's great mercy for salvation, but we get to rely on his wisdom as we walk through life.

Today, remember to ask God for guidance. He longs to teach you and lead you through life. He wants to walk with you through every moment of joy and frustration. He loves it when you turn to him and ask him for direction. If you ask, he will be faithful to lead you well.

Father, teach me your ways so that I will walk in them all of my days. Lead me on paths that are pleasing to you.

NO CONDEMNATION

There is therefore now no condemnation
for those who are in Christ Jesus.

ROMANS 8:1 ESV

In a society that loves justice, it can be difficult for us to understand what it means to live without condemnation. We love to see people pay the price for their wrongs. This is ironic because as Christians, our eternal security comes from us being completely unable to pay the price for our own wrongs. Those who believe that Jesus is the one and only Son of God, who repent of their sins, and who live to follow him, will never face condemnation.

You have been set free by the blood of Jesus. You don't have to live under the weight of sin because Jesus has paid the price for you. No matter the mistakes you have made, there is no need to get lost in guilt, shame, or embarrassment. In Christ, you will never face the punishment that you deserve. Instead, you receive unmerited favor for eternity.

Jesus, how can I ever thank you enough for your sacrifice? Help me to live without condemnation.

SUFFERING

Since we are his children, we are his heirs. In fact, together with Christ we are heirs of God's glory. But if we are to share his glory, we must also share his suffering.

ROMANS 8:17 NLT

When we are sharing Christ with others, we must be careful to be completely truthful about what it entails. Accepting Jesus as our Savior does not solve all our problems. There will still be trials, tribulations, and consequences as we live in a sinful world. We do others a disservice when we make it seem like the Christian life is devoid of suffering. The truth is that we will potentially suffer more because of our faith.

Have you embraced the suffering of Christ in your own life? Scripture is clear that you cannot share in his glory without sharing in his suffering. Trials and struggles will bring you closer to God if you let them. Don't shy away from difficult seasons but remember that they are a defining factor of the Christian life.

Jesus, I want to join you in your suffering. Help me to be courageous when difficult things happen.

HOW MUCH LONGER

What we suffer now is nothing
compared to the glory he will reveal to us later.

Romans 8:18 NLT

Have you witnessed the joy and expectation on your grandkids' faces as they anticipate an exciting family outing? Maybe it was a trip to a water park or an adventure hike. They knew what was waiting for them, and they envisioned all the fun they would have. They continually ask their parents how much longer they will have to wait until the special day finally arrives. Waiting seems like agony, but you know that it will be worth it.

Just like a child anxious for an adventure, wait expectantly for the return of Jesus. It is hard to wait for something that we know will be so incredibly good. We cannot wait for him to wipe away our tears and make all the wrong things right. Sometimes the trials we face while we wait seem unbearable, but we know that it will be worth it when he returns.

Jesus, thank you for your great plan of redemption. Help me to persevere as I wait for Chrit's return.

CONSTANT HELPER

The Spirit also helps our weakness; for we do not know what to pray for as we should, but the Spirit himself intercedes for us with groanings too deep for words.

ROMANS 8:26 NASB

Sometimes we find it difficult to pray. God knew this would happen, so he gave us a helper. His Holy Spirit lives in us and takes over when we are weak. When we don't have anything left to give, the Holy Spirit prays for us. When tears flow and the words are hard to find, we can trust that we are still seen and heard.

Don't let weakness prevent you from communicating with God. In times when you are too overwhelmed to speak, let the Holy Spirit advocate for you. He knows the deepest corners of your heart and can speak on your behalf. Instead of being discouraged, remember that you have a great helper who is eager to draw you close to the Lord.

Jesus, thank you for your Holy Spirit, my helper and intercessor. Help me to rely on the Spirit when I don't know how to pray.

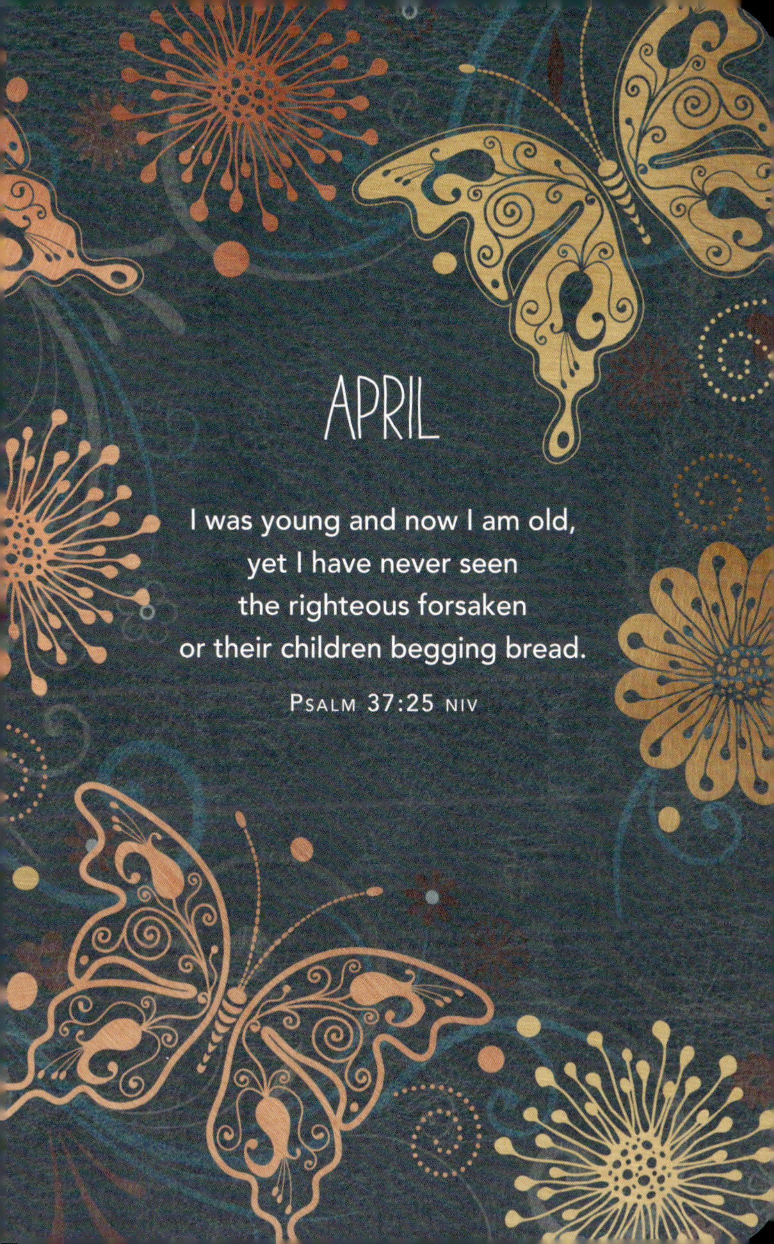

APRIL

I was young and now I am old,
yet I have never seen
the righteous forsaken
or their children begging bread.

Psalm 37:25 niv

GOOD PLANS

In everything God works for the good of those who love him. They are the people he called, because that was his plan.

ROMANS 8:28 NCV

It can be difficult to embrace the truth of God's goodness when trouble arises. We don't see the good in our suffering, nor do we understand why God allows it. One day we will see the big picture, fully understanding all that God has planned and aligned. Until then, we live by faith and trust that God is working everything out for our good because we love him.

Maybe your grandparenting experience hasn't been what you hoped. Maybe you have strained relationships with your children or are worried about the choices that they are making. Maybe the second half of your life looks vastly different than you expected. No matter what, God is still sovereign in your life. He has numbered your days, and you aren't finished yet. Trust that you aren't excluded from his goodness. He will keep all his promises.

Father, help me to trust in your faithfulness. I know that your plans for me are good.

HE DEFENDS US

If God is for us,
who can be against us?

ROMANS 8:31 ESV

A good father takes care of his children. He notices when they are hurt. He comforts them when they are sad. He pays attention to the possibility of danger, and he ensures that under his watch, each of his children is well tended to. Children feel secure in the presence of a good father. They know that no matter what they are afraid of, their dad can handle it.

Fear not! When doubts creep in or it seems like the world is against you, know that God is the absolute best Father. His love and protection surround you, giving you the strength you need for each day. No matter what you encounter, God is on your side. Just as you've spent your life caring for your loved ones with tenderness and grace, God cares for you even more deeply.

Father, thank you for being on my side. Thank you for your protection and attentiveness.

COUNT THE COST

Calling the crowd to join his disciples, he said, "If any of you wants to be my follower, you must give up your own way, take up your cross, and follow me."

Mark 8:34 NLT

We all grow up with high hopes for the future. Sometimes our wildest dreams come true, and sometimes we let them go. Either way, our greatest goal is to follow Christ's plan for our lives. We faithfully ask him to lead us, and he doesn't let us down. Life doesn't always look as we imagined it but that doesn't mean it isn't good.

As a grandmother, you've probably watched, or will watch, your grandchildren struggle through the formative years of their faith. You want only the best for them, and you know that the best means giving up their preferences in favor of what God has for them. For some this will mean a radical change of course and for others it won't. Either way, you can pray for each of your grandchildren to have soft hearts and a willingness to follow Jesus no matter the cost.

Father, help my grandchildren to count the cost and follow you no matter the sacrifice.

NO SEPARATION

Nothing can ever separate us from God's love. Neither death nor life, neither angels nor demons, neither our fears for today nor our worries about tomorrow—not even the powers of hell can separate us from God's love.

ROMANS 8:38 NLT

Some of us have experienced the panic that comes from momentarily losing sight of a child or grandchild. Immediately we have thoughts of where they are or who they might be with. Even a brief separation feels extraordinarily long. Little children are not meant to be apart from those who care for them and keep them safe.

In the same way, you are not meant to be separated from your good father. It is good for you to be close to him. Thankfully, you have the assurance that God never lets you out of his sight. There is nothing that can pull you away from his presence or deter his love for you. No matter how lost you may feel, you are never alone and never forsaken. Like a good father, he is always aware of you.

Father, thank you for your constant presence in my life.

REJOICE ALWAYS

This is the day the LORD has made;
We will rejoice and be glad in it.

PSALM 118:24 NKJV

Whether we wake up to sunshine or rain, the day is good. Whether we had a full night's sleep or a restless one, the day is good. Each new morning is a gift from God. No matter what comes our way, we can rejoice in what God has done. He has given us life and breath so we can relish every minute he blesses us with.

This exact day has been planned for you since before you were created. Today, you have every reason to celebrate and worship your great God and King. Commit your day to him and ask the Holy Spirit to lead you. Trust that he knows what every moment holds and how you can best glorify him. God has good things in store for you today!

Father, thank you for another day of life. I commit my time to you and want to honor you with each moment.

A NEW WAY

Christ is the mediator of a new covenant, that those who are called may receive the promised eternal inheritance—now that he has died as a ransom to set them free from the sins committed under the first covenant.

HEBREWS 9:15 NIV

Christ is the only way man can be forgiven once and for all, without punishment or condemnation. The weight of our sin is too great, and we cannot carry it on our own. Instead, Jesus carries it for us. He relieves us of our burdens and makes a way for us to be close to God.

Your chief purpose is to be near to God. This is what you were created for. This is what your soul longs for and what brings you true satisfaction and fulfillment. Jesus is the only reason that you can achieve that closeness. His sacrifice is what allows you to approach God's throne with confidence, knowing that you are made righteous. Don't hesitate today, thank Jesus for his sacrifice and find fullness of joy in God's presence.

Thank you, Jesus, for your free gift of forgiveness, salvation, and eternal life.

PERFECTLY MADE

"Who are you, a mere human being, to argue with God? Should the thing that was created say to the one who created it, 'Why have you make me like this?'"

ROMANS 9:20 NLT

If pressed, we could all make a list of things we are dissatisfied with. There are probably things we would change about ourselves or our circumstances if given the chance. It's easy to pick ourselves apart and assume we would be better, life would be better, if only a few things were different.

Do you ever feel this way? Are you the grandma you hoped you would be? Are you wishing things were different or better? The reality is that you are not equipped to know what is best for yourself. God, in his infinite wisdom, made you in a specific and intentional way. It isn't your job to decide that he cut corners or didn't finish the job. Instead, ask him to show you how to glorify him in a way that is specific to who you are.

Father, help me trust that you always know what is best for me. I don't want to question what you've done.

MEET THEM

When I am with those who are weak, I share their weakness, for I want to bring the weak to Christ. Yes, I try to find common ground with everyone, doing everything I can to save some.

1 CORINTHIANS 9:22 NLT

There are several times the Word outlines how we are meant to treat others. Paul shares the value that comes from meeting people where they are at. If someone is grieving, we are to meet them in their grief. If someone is joyful, we should share that joy. When we sincerely care for others and share in their emotions, we create an opportunity to love them the way that Christ loves them.

As a grandmother, you have endless opportunities to do this well. You can rejoice with your grandchildren when they are happy, and you can be near to them when they are sad. You can comfort them with your presence as they feel whatever they need to. You can be steady and constant no matter how they are feeling.

Jesus, help to meet my grandchildren where they are at. Teach me how to love like you do.

UNBELIEF

"Everything is possible for one who believes."

MARK 9:23 NIV

In this account, Jesus heals a boy who was possessed by a spirit. The father asks him to help *if he can*. When Jesus confronts the man's doubt, he responds courageously and declares that he believes Jesus can do anything. He goes on to ask for help with his unbelief. This is such a relatable position to be in. We believe that anything is possible for God but there are still areas where doubt can creep in. We should respond like the father in Mark, full of faith and yet dependent on God to handle our doubts.

Maybe you're waiting on God to do some big things in your family. Maybe you've been asking for help for a long time. Where your faith feels weak, Jesus is your strength. He will sustain you as you continuously go to him for help. Don't give up! Keep believing for miracles in your life.

Father, I believe that you are my strength. Increase my faith where I have unbelief.

FULL OF GRACE

"In the same way you judge others, you will be judged, and with the measure you use, it will be measured to you."

MATTHEW 7:2 NIV

It's easy, and sometimes fun, to judge others. We like to make observations about other people's lives and choices. Usually, judgement stems out of some sort of insecurity. It temporarily feels good to point out the flaws of others instead of fixing our own. It's important to remember that in the same way that we judge others, we will be judged. Do we want our harsh observations turned back on us? If the answer is no, it's time to rethink the way that we are treating those around us.

You might disagree with your children's parenting practices. Maybe you don't like the choices that your grandchildren are making. Maybe you disagree with the way your peers handle their own grandparenting season. No matter the situation, approach it with the same kindness and grace that you would want for yourself. Remember how you want to be treated amid your own mistakes and act from a place of understanding and empathy.

Father, help me not to cast judgement on others. I want to be merciful and empathetic.

HIS RETURN

Christ, having been offered once to bear the sins of many, will appear a second time, not to deal with sin but to save those who are eagerly waiting for him.

HEBREWS 9:28 ESV

The perfect Son of God chose death to pay for the sins of the world. He suffered so we can live. Jesus sacrificed himself so that we could be co-heirs with him. We no longer need to pay for our sins, and we are joyously welcomed into the kingdom of heaven. Now, we wait with expectation for him to come back again and make all things right.

Imagine the day of his return. Everything will be made perfect. You will operate exactly how you were made to. There will be no more doubt, worry, insecurity, fear, or confusion. Every circumstance in your life will perfectly glorify the one who made you. Every tear you've shed over disappointment or grief will be wiped away as you experience the wholeness and perfection of God's presence.

Jesus, help me to keep your return in my sights. I want to endure until you come back.

THE GREATEST

Sitting down, he called the Twelve and said to them, "If anyone wants to be first, he must be last and servant of all."

MARK 9:35 CSB

Upon arriving in Capernaum, Jesus asked his disciples what they were talking about on the journey. They were ashamed to tell him because they had been arguing about which of them was the greatest. Isn't that relatable? Each of us at times, have thought too highly of ourselves. Jesus shared with his disciples that to be first, they must consider others before themselves.

Motherhood, and now grandmotherhood, is full of opportunities to do this. Each day you can put the needs of your family before your own, knowing full well that God will take care of you. He is attentive to your cries and knows exactly what you need. You don't have to care for others out of a deficit but out of the abundance that God's love provides. Ask the Holy Spirit to help you serve your family with humility and love.

Jesus, help me serve you by serving others. I don't want to fight to be the best in my own eyes.

NOT A BURDEN

"Whoever welcomes this little child in my name welcomes me; and whoever welcomes me welcomes the one who sent me. For it is the one who is least among you all who is the greatest."

LUKE 9:48 NIV

Most of us have eaten in a restaurant with our grandkids and noticed the people around us are not fans of children. Some people just don't tolerate children. Many people still think that children should be seen and not heard, but Jesus loves and welcomes them. In fact, when we are kind to a child, we are kind to Christ.

If you want to please your Father in heaven, treat children well. Value them and be kind toward them. As a grandmother, you have many opportunities to do this. Lavish love on your grandchildren. Shower them with affection and do all you can to make them feel like the most important person in the room. When you treat children as a blessing, not a burden, you honor God.

God, help me value all children the way that Jesus does. I want my grandchildren to feel loved, noticed, and accepted.

WISE CHILDREN

Wise children make their father happy,
but foolish children make their mother sad.

Proverbs 10:1 NCV

As grandparents, many of us have seen this verse come to fruition in our own lives. When our children make wise decisions, we are delighted and full of pride. When they make foolish decisions, we are distraught and sad. Every parent has experienced this, especially those of us with older children. When our children make wise decisions without our help, we rejoice and are so proud.

As you watch your adult children live apart from you, trust that God is leading them well. Pray that he will give them wisdom as they navigate adulthood. Ask God to help them make good decisions and watch with pride as they do their best to honor the Lord.

Father, thank you for the gift of my children. Help them to make wise decisions and to lean on you for guidance.

CAPTIVE THOUGHTS

We take captive every thought to make it obedient to Christ.

2 CORINTHIANS 10:5 NIV

Most of us are very aware of our own downfalls. We don't need someone to point out our failures. We know that we fall short of God's standard and probably feel guilty or ashamed of our weaknesses. Instead of focusing on our failures, we need to realize that we have been fully equipped to live in obedience to Christ. He does not ask us to do something impossible. He has provided us with everything we need for godliness.

When you find yourself falling into negative thought patterns, surrender them to Jesus. When you find yourself giving in to anxiety and fear, submit those fears to Jesus. What passes through your mind isn't what defines you. Instead, give it all to Christ and let him be glorified in your life.

Jesus, fill my mind with praise and worship for you. Help me to take my thoughts captive.

MIRACULOUS AND SIMPLE

If you declare with your mouth, "Jesus is Lord," and believe in your heart that God raised him from the dead, you will be saved.

Romans 10:9 NIV

Is there anything we want more for our grandkids than to hear them profess Jesus as their Lord and Savior? Everything else pales in comparison to the joy of knowing that they are walking with God. This is our highest hope for them. As such, we can teach them the miraculous simplicity of the gospel. Today's culture will paint it as complicated and condemning but we can testify that it is not.

Share the freedom of the gospel with your grandchildren. Tell them, again and again, that if they confess that Jesus is Lord and trust that Christ was raised from the dead, they will be saved. It isn't complicated or impossible. Following Jesus does not mean they are bound to an impractical list of rules that they must follow. Pray that the truth will take deep root within the hearts of your grandchildren.

Jesus, help me to share the beauty and simplicity of the gospel with my grandchildren.

THE THIEF

"The thief comes only to steal and kill and destroy. I came that they may have life and have it abundantly."

John 10:10 ESV

We go to great lengths to secure our safety. We install security systems and utilize doorbells with video cameras. We are very aware of our physical safety. Yet the greatest enemy we will ever face attacks our spirits and our souls. Satan is a thief who tries to tempt us, deconstruct our faith, and cause spiritual destruction amongst believers. He wants us to doubt and defy God's goodness.

There might be things in your life that you feel Satan has stolen from you. Remember that God is greater than the enemy's greatest schemes. There is nothing that God cannot redeem and restore. God wants you to have an abundant life, full of joy and peace in his presence. If you saturate your heart and minds with God's Word, you won't fall into the enemy's traps.

Jesus, help me to remember that you are always stronger than any enemy I might have.

ALWAYS SAFE

You go before me and follow me.
You place your hand of blessing on my head.

PSALM 139:5 NLT

God is the epitome of security. He knows when we arise and when we sleep. He knows every detail of our days and he promises to protect his children. He knows our comings and goings before we do. He goes ahead of us, preparing the way. He follows behind us and is our shield. When danger approaches, he hides us in the shadow of his wings.

Maybe as a grandparent you find yourself worrying a lot more than you anticipated. You're concerned about your grandchildren and only want what's best for them. Remember that God is their great protector. They too are his masterpiece and great delight. Just as God has been faithful to keep you safe, he will protect them. There is no protection that you can offer them that is greater than what God is constantly doing. Submit them into his hands and let him handle all your worries.

Father, thank you for a lifetime of protection. Help me to trust you with the safety of my grandkids.

FAITH OF A CHILD

"Whoever does not receive the kingdom of God like a child shall not enter it."

MARK 10:15 ESV

Can you imagine the response if a child offered a few cents to get into a yacht club or exclusive fitness center? They would be turned away and laughed at for assuming their pittance would gain them acceptance. This isn't the case with God's kingdom. In fact, anyone who doesn't proceed with the faith of a child will not gain entry. Anyone who tries to work or buy their salvation will learn that God's currency is different from ours.

You are asked to have the faith of a child to enter the kingdom of God. As a grandparent you have so many opportunities to see what that means! Watch your grandchildren. Observe their innocence and how they trust without condition. Learn from them and ask the Lord to give you more humility as you get older.

Jesus, help me to have childlike faith. Teach me about yourself through my grandkids.

YOU BELONG

We come closer to God and approach him with an open heart, fully convinced that nothing will keep us at a distance from him. For our hearts have been sprinkled with blood to remove impurity, and we have been freed from an accusing conscience.

HEBREWS 10:22 TPT

We are delighted by the presence of our grandchildren. We love it when they choose to be with us. Whether they want to share a silly anecdote or talk to us about a problem they're having, we are just so happy to be near to them. We long to embrace them, encourage them, and be part of their lives.

In the same way, God longs for you to be near to him. You can approach him with an open heart, fully convinced you belong. You don't need to go to him in embarrassment, assuming he'll turn you away. As his child you will always be welcomed into his presence. Just like a doting grandparent with a beloved grandchild, God wants to near to you.

Father, thank you that I can approach you with confidence, knowing that I belong in your presence.

KIND CORRECTION

See if there is any offensive way in me
and lead me in the way everlasting.

Psalm 139:24 NIV

Most children, even toddlers, know if they are being disobedient. If little ones want to ignore a request, they'll turn their heads away and pretend they don't hear. The last thing they want to do is acknowledge their naughtiness. Sometimes, we as adults haven't grown past this habit either. No one likes to be confronted with their flaws and shortcomings. Yet, the Psalmist assures us that as we let God purify our hearts, we will find everlasting life.

You can trust God with your failures. He is always gentle and kind in the correction of his children. He is a good father who knows exactly what his children need. He is not harsh and condemning. Instead, he leads us perfectly along a path to sanctification, knowing exactly how to teach us to be more like him. You can always be open to God's correction because you know that he is not a harsh, egotistical teacher.

Father, search my heart and reveal any sins I am not acknowledging. Help me humbly repent, so I may live an upright life.

REMEMBER WHEN

"With people it is impossible, but not with God;
for all things are possible with God."

MARK 10:27 NASB

We've all faced impossible situations in life. Sometimes our jobs don't work out, our finances seem dismal, and our relationships just aren't what we'd hoped. Situations that seem impossible to us are not daunting to God. There is no conflict, trial, or trauma that he cannot help us navigate. With his help, we can walk through anything. We will be successful when we rely on his strength over our own.

Encourage your grandchildren that nothing is impossible for God. Share with them the trials that you have faced. You can be a calm voice of reason, reminding them that nothing is as bad as it seems, and that God can handle whatever they are facing. You can provide a source of steadiness when they are overwhelmed and full of disappointment. When life isn't working out the way they want, you can encourage them and meet them where they are at.

Father, thank you for using my testimony to encourage my grandchildren. Help me to lift them up with my words and remind them of your strength.

FOLLOW JESUS

Follow my example,
as I follow the example of Christ.

1 Corinthians 11:1 NIV

Paul, apostle and author of today's verse, encourages us to follow his example. Yet what he really means is that his readers should follow the life of Christ. There is a distinction to be made. We are not meant to follow Paul, or any man, if they are not also following Jesus. It's common to get caught up in trusting a leader to use discernment all the while forsaking our own. We should use caution in who we choose to follow.

Just as you pick your influences carefully, remember that your grandchildren are watching you. As they follow you, ensure that you are also following Jesus. At the end of the day, his authority and direction matter far more than yours. The end goal of leading is family is not that they are obedient to you but that they are obedient to Jesus.

Jesus, help me to follow you closely as my family follows me.

APRIL 24

Love finds no joy in unrighteousness but rejoices in the truth.
It bears all things, believes all things, hopes all things,
endures all things.

1 Corinthians 13:6-7 CSB

As we seek to honor the Lord in all we do, we must learn how to love like he does. Scripture says that godly love has endurance. This means that we are meant to love well, even when it is difficult. If we follow worldly advice, we will love each other when it is convenient and comfortable. Godly love does not dissipate in the face of hardship or conflict. Rather, it endures and perseveres.

If you look at the relationships in your life, would you say that they have endurance? If the answer is no, then perhaps it is time to evaluate if you love others with your own strength. Instead of using your own abilities, rely on God's strength to love others when conflict arises.

Father, I want to love with endurance. I don't want to shy away from uncomfortable situations. Help me to love sacrificially.

FOUNDATIONAL FAITH

Without faith living within us it would be impossible to please God. For we come to God in faith knowing that he is real and that he rewards the faith of those who passionately seek him.

Hebrews 11:6 TPT

We cannot please God without faith. This is because faith is required even to believe in the mere existence of God. We must rely on what we cannot see to follow the Lord. We must look past what makes sense to the world and trust what we cannot always prove. Our belief in his existence is foundational. How can we serve God well if we aren't convinced that he is real?

Great faith can only be accomplished through the power of God. If you ask him to grow your faith, he will. As you lean into the power and the teaching of the Word, you will believe more and more that God is reliable and good. As you trust in his goodness, your actions will reflect your beliefs.

Father, I want my faith to be steady and strong. I don't want to waver in my belief of your existence or your goodness.

LIFT UP

A gossip betrays a confidence,
but a trustworthy person keeps a secret.

PROVERBS 11:13 NIV

Gossip stems from an impure desire to elevate ourselves above other people. When we focus on the problems of others, we feel superior and vindicated. It is the most misguided type of communication because it hurts everyone involved. There is no winner and there is nothing productive happening.

People notice when the only thing you like to talk about is other people. As a result, you might notice that they don't share the details of their life with you. Your gossip has proven that you cannot be trusted. Instead, seek to be the kind of woman who only lifts others up. Be the kind of mother and grandmother who is esteemed for the way that she speaks. Ask God to help you to discipline your tongue. The more you use your words to encourage, the stronger that muscle will become.

Father, I want my thoughts and words to honor you. Help me to focus on lifting others up.

MANY COUNSELORS

Where there is no guidance the people fall,
but in abundance of counselors there is victory.

PROVERBS 11:14 NASB

We are not meant to walk through life alone. Left to our own devices, we don't always make the best choices. Scripture warns that we will fall without guidance. Instead, we should embrace the wisdom of others and the counsel of the godly. This allows us to make well rounded decisions that are based on more than our own biased opinions. It is good to humbly ask for help and guidance.

As you practice seeking godly counsel, your grandchildren will see that it is good and right to ask for help. Your example of humility will not go unnoticed. Ask often for the opinions of others. Listen to what they have to say and with the Holy Spirit's discernment, take their words into account. As you embrace having many counselors, you open yourself up to wisdom that you may not have seen otherwise.

Jesus, help me to embrace the practice of asking for help.

GIFT OF GATHERING

I will thank the LORD with all my heart
as I meet with his godly people.

PSALM 111:1 NLT

It's easy to take church for granted in a country that does not condemn us for going. We aren't always faithful to meet with believers because we know that we'll always have another opportunity. Sometimes laziness, offense, and pride get in the way of being together consistently. Surely our perspective would be different if the right to meet were taken away from us. The fact that we can corporately encourage each other and seek discipleship is a treasure.

Are you part of a healthy community of believers? If the answer is no, ask God to help you find one. It's just as important to him as it is to you. When you don't meet with the body of Christ you miss out on the shared love, unity and fellowship that comes with it. You were not meant to endure alone.

Father, help me to embrace the gift of meeting with other believers. I'm so grateful that we can gather and worship you.

DISPLAY KINDNESS

Kind people do themselves a favor,
but cruel people bring trouble on themselves.

PROVERBS 11:17 NCV

In a world that prioritizes success and self-preservation, remember that scripture emphasizes the importance of being kind. Even small acts of kindness can have a big impact. When we practice putting the needs of others first, we are doing ourselves a favor. We are spreading truth and warmth which will in turn have a positive impact on our own lives. A kind heart is light and at ease while a cruel heart is troubled and distraught.

As a grandmother you are a source of comfort, kindness, and warmth. The way you treat your grandchildren can impact future generations. You can spread joy and reflect the love of Christ to your family. Ask God to show you new ways to be kind to your grandchildren. He will help you be creative and heartfelt in the way that you love them.

Father, I want to shower my family with kindness. Help me to love them like you do.

GREAT FAITH

"I tell you, whatever you ask for in prayer, believe that you have received it, and it will be yours."

MARK 11:24 NIV

When we pray, are we assured that our good father hears? Or do we continue to doubt, even after a lifetime of witnessing his faithfulness? Jesus was clear, those who ask and believe will receive. If we believe God doesn't answer our prayers, our commitment to prayer will wane and eventually die. But if we are filled with faith, our prayer life will be vibrant, expectant, and earnest.

How would you describe your prayer life? If you are satisfied, go in peace, and continue to commune with your creator. If you are dissatisfied or ashamed, lift your head and go to him with humility. He will never shame you or scold you for a lack of faith. Instead, he will lead you gently and encourage you. Ask him to increase your faith and let your prayers be bold and from the heart.

Father, increase my faith and help me have a vibrant prayer life.

MAY

They will still bear fruit in old age,
they will stay fresh and green.

Psalm 92:14 NIV

MINE

Give freely and become more wealthy;
be stingy and lose everything.

Proverbs 11:24 NLT

We've all seen our grandchildren refuse to share their toys. We think this is childish behavior that will be outgrown. Even if we learn how to share beyond our toddler sized capacity, we carry some level of selfishness into adulthood. The toys we keep to ourselves are just bigger now. Whether we hoard plastic school buses or nice houses with big yards, the heart of the matter is the same.

It can be scary to ask God to reveal areas of selfishness. If you do, he will surely show you areas where you can be more generous. As you embrace generosity, he will be faithful to take care of you. Scripture is clear that the giver often receives as well. As a grandparent, you can give with abundance no matter your financial situation. Seek to glorify God with your attitude and your resources.

Father, forgive me for the times I've been stingy with my blessings. Help me to be generous.

FULLY QUALIFIED

"I thank you, Father, Lord of heaven and earth, that you have hidden these things from the wise and understanding and revealed them to little children."

MATTHEW 11:25 ESV

Jesus didn't walk the earth in a manner that was expected. Most people expected a mighty king who would wage battle against their oppressors. Instead, they got a ragged group of fishermen, largely uneducated and unsophisticated. The twelve men Jesus chose revolutionized the way people saw their Messiah. God was setting the precedence that he doesn't operate in the ways of the world.

There may be times as a grandmother that you feel ill equipped. Maybe you don't think you have what it takes to pour into your grandchildren or support your children in their parenting. Maybe you feel too impatient, too tired, or too overwhelmed. This is good news! Your weakness provides space for God's strength to shine through. All through history he has used the weak and ill equipped to accomplish his will.

God, thank you for using the childish and ill equipped. Help me to lean on your strength.

RECEIVE HIS REST

"Come to me, all you who are weary and burdened,
and I will give you rest."

MATTHEW 11:28 NIV

As we get older, we notice new aches and pains. Our bodies don't operate the way they used to, and we are very aware of our new weaknesses. Not only do we experience some new physical limitations, but we also have new mental and emotional challenges as we age.

Remember that no matter your burden or weakness, Jesus offers rest. Whether your body is tired, or your emotions are overwhelming, Jesus is the answer. Bring your problems to him and lay them at his feet. He doesn't want you to go through your days weary and exhausted. Instead, he desires that you would rest at his feet, trusting that he will always take care of you.

Jesus, thank you for your rest and peace, both now and in eternity.

CLEAN HEART

Create in me a clean heart, O God,
and renew a right spirit within me.

Psalm 51:10 ESV

David was guilty of adultery with Bathsheba and the murder of her husband, Uriah. He knew that he was wrong, and he wasted no time repenting. He immediately fasted and spoke the words of this psalm. His conversation with God is an example of deep repentance for all of us to emulate. Like David, we should respond immediately when we recognize our sin. We should go to God with true humility and sorrow for our transgressions.

In your times with the Lord, ask him to give you a sensitive spirit. Then, when you sin, you won't be blinded by your own pride. A willingness to admit when you are wrong paves the way toward peace and restoration. When you make mistakes, run to him with confidence, knowing that he is merciful and loves to forgive his children.

Father, soften my heart. Help me to be aware of my sin. I want to repent quickly and run to you with confidence.

GOOD EXAMPLES

Since we are surrounded by such a great cloud of witnesses, let us throw off everything that hinders and the sin that so easily entangles. And let us run with perseverance the race marked out for us.

HEBREWS 12:1 NIV

God's Word is filled with accounts of people being obedient to God. Although the stories vary, typically their journeys weren't easy. As they depended on God for deliverance, they found victory. They had faith to follow him with undivided hearts. They did not trust in their own understanding but acknowledged God's ways and walked in them.

When you are discouraged, you can look to these stories to bolster your faith. They can remind you that if God kept his promises then, he will do it again. As you are encouraged by the lives of others, remember that your life can also serve as a testimony to God's goodness. Your grandchildren will one day look back and see how God was faithful to you. How wonderful would it be if you were counted in their great cloud of witnesses.

Father, thank you for so many encouraging stories. Strengthen my faith and help me to be an example to others of your goodness.

LOVE CORRECTION

To learn, you must love discipline;
it is stupid to hate correction.

Proverbs 12:1 NLT

We are all born into sin. No one needs to teach us to do wrong. We are all equal in our propensity to make mistakes. Without God's kind reproof, we would be lost. It would be ridiculous for us to insist that we are always right and refuse the good and right correction of the Lord.

The ability to gracefully accept correction is not something that you learn once and are done with. It's a muscle that must be continuously exercised. Ask God to give you a humble heart and the grace to accept when you are wrong. Age is not a qualifier for rightness. Instead, daily ask God to help you stay open to correction.

Father, thank you for loving me enough to correct me. Help me to be humble and open to growth no matter how old I am.

ONLY GOD

Since God has shown us great mercy, I beg you to offer your lives as a living sacrifice to him. Your offering must be only for God and pleasing to him.

ROMANS 12:1 NCV

God is the only one who can offer us mercy and salvation. Our salvation should result in a desire to gratefully serve God. He is worthy of everything we have to offer. As such, everything we do should be motivated by serving God wholeheartedly, not impressing those around us. If we are working for the praise of men, we will surely fail.

In the later years of your life, you may be tempted to prove that you have done well. You may want the people around you to notice your success and think highly of your accomplishments. After all, you've probably worked really heard. Instead, your standard for success should be God's opinion. His voice matters most.

Father, I want my life to be a pleasant offering to you and you alone. I don't want to work for the praise of those around me.

DON'T BE CONFORMED

Do not be shaped by this world; instead be changed within by a new way of thinking. Then you will be able to decide what God wants for you; you will know what is good and pleasing to him and what is perfect.

ROMANS 12:2 NCV

We are constantly being told how to live and what we need to be happy. The world wants us to continuously chase personal satisfaction and yet it seems like it is never found. The world misleads us, but God's Word speaks truth. Scripture tells us to not be conformed to this world. The drive for pleasure and immediate gratification are displeasing to God.

As a grandparent, you may find yourself in the season of retirement. It is good and right to rest well after years of hard work. Keep in mind that a well-deserved season of rest doesn't necessarily equate with a season of endless satisfaction. Even in later years, you should still follow the Lord's leadership when it comes to how you live. God still asks you to embrace humility, generosity, and servant hearted leadership.

Father, help me to continue to honor you in my later years. I don't want to fall into the trap of chasing personal satisfaction.

GODLY MARRIAGE

An excellent wife is the crown of her husband,
but she who causes shame is like rottenness in his bones.

PROVERBS 12:4 NKJV

A godly wife is the joy of her husband. She lifts him up and doesn't cause him shame. He is confident because she respects and cares for him. She loves God first, and her husband and family second. She seeks the Lord, prays for her loved ones, and lives an upright life. An excellent wife is a treasure to be cherished.

Today, ask God to be glorified in your marriage. If you are not married, ask him to be glorified in the marriages of your adult children. A godly marriage has a positive impact on the entire family. It's a reflection of the way Christ loves the church, and it displays what sacrificial love really looks like.

Father, help me be a good wife who honors her husband. Bless the marriages of my family members. Help them to glorify you.

EMBRACE DISCIPLINE

Have you completely forgotten this word of encouragement that addresses you as a father addresses his son? It says, "My son, do not make light of the Lord's discipline, and do not lose heart when he rebukes you."

HEBREWS 12:5 NIV

When God disciplines his children, it is because he loves us. He wants what is best for us and he knows how and when to correct us. His discipline is always gentle, kind, and patient. He is not waiting for us to mess up and he is not harsh or demanding in his correction. Everything he does has a purpose, and we can trust that he is capable of helping us grow in our faith.

Don't be discouraged when God disciplines you. Don't assume that you aren't good enough or that you just don't measure up. None of those things are true. The truth is that his discipline is evidence of his great love for you. He loves you too much to let you continue on a path that leads to destruction or death. No matter how uncomfortable it is, rejoice when you see an area of your life that needs to change.

Father, help me to embrace your discipline in my life. I know that you love me and know what's best.

SINCERE LOVE

Love must be sincere. Hate what is evil; cling to what is good.

ROMANS 12:9 NIV

We can tell when our grandchildren behave lovingly only because they want something. Learning how to get what we want is inherent to being human. We are born with the tendency to manipulate others to get what we want. However, just because we are born with it, doesn't mean we should continue down that path of behavior. Our love is meant to be sincere and honest. We are supposed to love others because God loves us, not just to get something we want.

Today, take some time to evaluate your intentions with the help of the Holy Spirit. Ask if there are areas of your life that are inauthentic or self-serving. If he highlights something, respond with humility and seek to behave differently. If you ask him for help, God will faithfully teach you how to love others well.

Jesus, help me to love others with sincerity. I don't want to behave like a child, manipulating others to get my way. Help me to mature in love.

LEARN WELL

Our parents disciplined us for a little while as they thought best; but God disciplines us for our good, in order that we may share in his holiness.

Hebrews 12:10 NIV

We hope that our grandchildren will be raised with healthy boundaries and consistent correction.

Without training in righteousness, our grandchildren are left to their own devices and pervasive sinful nature. We hope that they will grow up with soft hearts, open to the correction of both their parents and their heavenly Father.

Just as you hope to see healthy discipline in your grandchildren's lives, remember that you yourself are never too old for correction. There is never a season in which you can declare yourself better off without God's teaching and guidance. Your need for discipline will always be present. Embrace humility and learn well, just as you hope your grandchildren will.

Father, help me humbly accept your discipline so it will produce fruit in me. Help me to embrace learning and correction at every age.

DEVOTED TO LOVE

Be devoted to tenderly loving your fellow believers as members of one family. Try to outdo yourselves in respect and honor of one another.

Romans 12:10 TPT

Listening to our young grandchildren reveals how prone we all are to selfishness. They fight, complain, and demand their own way. Loving others well is not something we are born with and it's not something that changes just because we decide to follow Jesus. Loving others well takes discipline and intentionality. Scripture says we must be *devoted* to tenderly loving other believers. This implies that it's something that requires work and can be obtained over time.

If you struggle with selfishness, take heart, God can help you transform your ways. Lean into him and ask him for opportunities to love others well. He will teach you how to be tender and gentle just like he is. As you experience his love more and more, you'll learn how to pass it on to others.

Jesus, help me love sacrificially as you did. I want to grow in the way that I love others. Help me to be devoted to tenderness and kindness.

GODLY DISCIPLINE

No discipline seems pleasant at the time, but painful. Later on, however, it produces a harvest of righteousness and peace for those who have been trained by it.

Hebrews 12:11 NIV

As parents we know that healthy discipline reaps generous rewards. We know the value of discipline and hope that our grown children embrace the same truth as they raise their children. Watching our adult children discipline their children wrongly, or refuse to do it at all, can be one of the most difficult parts of being a grandparent.

Knowing that God values healthy discipline, you can pray that your children will honor him in how they treat their children. When they struggle as parents, humbly offer help. Pray for them consistently and remind them that you are proud to be on their team. Offer encouragement and support when they need it most.

Father, thank you for the fruit that comes from discipline. Help my adult children to discipline well.

ERADICATE PRIDE

Though the LORD is great, he cares for the humble,
but he keeps his distance from the proud.

PSALM 138:6 NLT

God hates pride. When we are filled with pride, we are unaware of our need for God. Without God we are helplessly lost and are bound by our own sin. If we want to embrace what is best for us, we must first be aware of our own needs. This cannot happen when pride is clouding our judgement.

Pride is sneaky and is often present in your life without you realizing it. This is why asking the Holy Spirit for discernment is so necessary. Ask him to show you where you have let pride into your heart and then respond with quick repentance. As you consistently surrender your will to God, eradicating pride from your life will become habitual.

Father, help me to embrace humility and be diligent to keep pride from my life. I know that I am always in need of you and your help.

WORK HARD

Do not be lazy but work hard,
serving the Lord with all your heart.

ROMANS 12:11 NCV

No matter what our job is, we are called do all our tasks with excellence and a desire to glorify God. It doesn't matter if we are doing physical labor, sitting at a desk or caring for others, everything we do should be done unto the Lord. When we work hard, we honor him.

Whether you are at the height of your career, have long since retired, or have cared for your family full time, you can honor God with the way that you work. No matter your season of life, you can pursue excellence and diligence in how you spend your time. Look for areas in your life where you may have cut corners and seek to change your habits. It is never too late. You can always adjust.

Father, please convict me when I am lazy. I want to do my best for you. Show me how I can embrace hard work in all that I do.

HELP MY UNBELIEF

Immediately the boy's father exclaimed, "I do believe; help me overcome my unbelief!"

Mark 9:24 NIV

We are quick to confess that God can do miraculous things. We want to have strong faith and believe that he will do great things. This is good but it is also good to admit that sometimes we have doubts. God is not intimidated by our doubts. Struggling to believe something does not make us less successful as Christians. Instead of viewing doubt as a weakness, we should simply hand it over to God.

When doubt creeps into your life, you can simply take notice of it and give it to God. Picture pulling weeds in a garden. You're not distraught every time you find another intruder. The presence of weeds in your garden doesn't make you a horrible gardener. You simply pluck it out and toss it aside. Treat doubts the same way. Hand them over, and let God deal with it.

Father, help me to trust you with my doubts. When I struggle to believe the truth, help me to lean on you instead of being discouraged.

GENEROSITY AND HOSPITALITY

When God's people are in need, be ready to help them.
Always be eager to practice hospitality.

Romans 12:13 NLT

We are to love our brothers and sisters above ourselves. To do that, we must be willing to give and do whatever it takes to help them. Our willingness to be generous is a direct reflection of how we view the blessings that we have. Every good thing in our lives is gift from God and we should treat it as such. We should remain open-handed and willing to share.

Do you find yourself coming up with reasons not to be generous? If the answer is yes, ask God to change your heart. He loves to give abundantly and will always take care of you when you do the same. When he asks you to be generous, he will not leave you empty handed.

Father, help me excel in generosity and hospitality. I don't want to hoard your blessings for myself.

PEACEFUL RELATIONSHIPS

Make every effort to live in peace with everyone and to be holy; without holiness no one will see the Lord.

HEBREWS 12:14 NIV

We are supposed to make every effort to maintain peaceful relationships with others. We can only do this by the power of God. We must depend on him and follow the leading of the Holy Spirit. As we walk forth with the fruit of the spirit, people around us will learn about God's character. When our relationships are defined by patience, kindness, gentleness, and self-control, others will see God.

It is never too late to see God work for good in your relationships. He can redeem even the most broken and tired relationship. Submit to his ways and ask him how to move forward. Embrace humility and make consistent effort to live peacefully with those around you.

Father, help me seek peace in all situations. I want my relationships to glorify you.

CHOOSE WELL

"Choose for yourselves this day whom you will serve."

JOSHUA 24:15 NKJV

No one is an accidental slave. We all choose who our master is. If we don't prioritize serving the Lord, we will inevitably place something else on the throne of our lives. We will bow down to wealth, acceptance, fame, or some other worldly promise. We each have the power to choose what or whom we will serve.

You get to decide where your allegiance lies. Will you be a slave to money, to the opinions of others, or to political ideas instead of God? He wants to have first place in your life. This is not because he is a greedy or tyrannical leader. Instead, it's because he knows what is best for you and loves you dearly.

Father, I choose you now and forever. I want to serve you and only you. Help me to arrange my priorities.

LISTEN WELL

The way of fools seems right to them,
but the wise listen to advice.

PROVERBS 12:15 NIV

We've all tried to reason with a grandchild who refused to sway from their opinion. Sometimes, children cannot be reasoned with. We give allowances for immaturity, but have we asked ourselves if we are prone to the same stubbornness? Just because we are older doesn't mean that we are immune to the pitfalls of the young.

Do you readily listen to the advice of others or are you convinced that your opinion is best? It is wise to take into consideration the ideas and perspectives of others. God has blessed each of his children in different ways. We embrace unity when we value the wisdom of others.

Father, open my eyes to the wisdom of others. Help me to listen well and embrace wisdom.

TAKE NOTICE

Be happy with those who are happy,
and weep with those who weep.

ROMANS 12:15 NLT

We are meant to approach the emotions of others with awareness. To be happy with those who are happy and to weep with those who weep, we must first pay attention. We need to open our eyes and turn our thoughts outward instead of inward. If we are too busy thinking about ourselves and our own problems, we won't notice how anyone else is doing.

Being thoughtful takes practice. If this isn't something that comes naturally to you, you can exercise it like a muscle. Ask God to help you notice one person today. Ask him to open your eyes to the joys or sorrows of a friend. The more you train yourself to see beyond your own life, the easier it becomes.

Lord, help me to be sensitive to the needs of others. I don't want to spend my life focused on myself.

EMBRACE MERCY

Never pay back evil with more evil. Do things in such a way that everyone can see you are honorable.

ROMANS 12:17 NLT

Do not repay evil with evil. As followers of Jesus, we are meant to rise above the actions of others. Vindication and revenge have no place in the life of the believer. We all desire justice but it is not our job to seek it out. Instead, we leave judgement in the hands of God and trust that one day, he will make all things right.

There have likely been times in your life when you have been treated unfairly. It's likely that there will be more to come. It's in those moments that your character is tested. You can dwell on what you cannot change, or you can lean on the Lord and trust his ways. You yourself have received great mercy when you didn't deserve it. Instead of seething with frustration, try to extend some of that mercy to your own wrongdoers.

Father, help me forgive as you forgive me. When I am wronged, help me to embrace mercy.

SPEAK WISELY

Careless words stab like a sword,
but wise words bring healing.

PROVERBS 12:18 NCV

If we spend any amount of time on social media, we'll quickly see how prevalent careless words are in our culture. Many people are either unaware or are uncaring of the impact their words can have. As followers of Jesus, we are called to behave differently. Our words should be intentional, kind, and full of love.

Your words have a strong impact on your family. You can encourage your adult children and praise them for the way that they parent. You can speak life over your grandchildren and shower them love and affection. Your words are powerful.

Lord, help me think before I speak. Show me the power of my words and help me to bring healing to my family.

LIVE AT PEACE

If it is possible, as far as it depends on you,
live at peace with everyone.

Romans 12:18 NIV

Living at peace with others is easier said than done. In order to truly live at peace with those around us, we must be willing to lay down our own expectations and agendas. This can especially be true within our own families. There are times when what we want needs to come second to the wants and needs of others.

As a mother and now a grandmother, you are surely used to laying your life down for others. Just because your children are grown doesn't mean that your role as peacemaker is over. God still calls you to work at living peacefully with your adult children.

Father, show me how to live at peace with those around me. I want to honor you by loving my family well.

SPEAK LIFE

Anxious fear brings depression,
but a life-giving word of encouragement
can do wonders to restore joy to the heart.

PROVERBS 12:25 TPT

Being anxious cannot help our current situation. Spending valuable time and energy ruminating over something we can't change will never bring about a solution. Instead, Scripture outlines that an encouraging word can abolish anxiety and bring joy. We can seek this out for ourselves and be aware of when others need encouragement.

The next time you find yourself struggling with anxiety, ask for help. Share your fears with a friend and ask for encouragement. A lot of anxiety's power lies in isolation. When we invite others into our lives, we open ourselves up to their wisdom and encouragement.

Father, help me to seek out the encouragement of others when I need it. I don't want to isolate myself and get lost in anxiety.

STEADY AND SECURE

Since we are receiving a kingdom that cannot be shaken, let us be thankful, and so worship God acceptably with reverence and awe.

HEBREWS 12:28 NIV

We live in a time that can sometimes feel shaky and unsteady. Everything is so fast paced. By the time we get our heads around one change, something even bigger is happening. It seems like nothing is stable, nothing is sacred, and nothing is secure. We long for simplicity, quietness, and calm. Instead, we are daily faced with calamity and chaos.

Maybe the ever-changing culture makes you feel like you have whiplash. Maybe the later years of life have left you with some big questions. Maybe some key parts of your life feel unsettled or unsure. No matter what is keeping you from feeling secure, remember that you are receiving a kingdom that cannot be moved. For every ounce of uncertainty you feel in this life, Christ will hold you steadfast for a million moments more.

Thank you, Father, that you and your kingdom cannot be shaken. Help me to feel steady even when the world around me is shaking.

TREASURES ON EARTH

"Where your treasure is,
there your heart will be also."

LUKE 12:34 NIV

Whether we like it or not, our finances are often very telling of the state of our hearts. If we want to know someone's priorities, simply look at where they spend their money. We won't buy things we don't value, and we won't skimp on the things we do. It might be tempting to spend our later years indulging in some of the things we've gone without but it's important that we are still submitting our finances to God even if our working years are over.

Each paycheck is an opportunity to ask God's opinion about your finances. Maybe you're in a season of worry and you don't know what the future holds. Maybe you're in a season of abundance and have plenty to spare. The specifics of your situation don't matter as much as how you are handling it. Remember that you cannot store treasure on Earth. Instead, be obedient to invest in what is eternal.

Father, help me to put your opinion first when it comes to my finances.

SUBMIT TO AUTHORITY

Everyone must submit to governing authorities. For all authority comes from God, and those in positions of authority have been placed there by God.

ROMANS 13:1 NLT

A lot of us prickle at the mention of submitting to authority. We don't like to be told what to do, and we certainly don't like to be governed by someone we don't agree with. We can speculate about nuances, but scripture is clear, we should respect those in authoritative positions. Disagreeing isn't grounds for rudeness, name calling, or stirring up offense. Instead, as followers of Christ we should esteem everyone as greater than ourselves.

As a grandparent, you've likely seen a lot of political turmoil over the span of your life. You've seen governments rise and fall, families fight over who's right, and friends break off relationships over differing opinions. Have you taken time to humbly submit this area of your life to God? Ask him how he would like you to think and act. He will be faithful to lead you in a direction that is life giving and God honoring.

Father, I want to honor you in all my ways. Help me to be respectful of authority.

ALWAYS AWARE

Remember to welcome strangers, because some who have done this have welcomed angels without knowing it.

HEBREWS 13:2 NCV

Most of us like to operate on our own terms. We want to be in control of our days, and we like to know what to expect. Unfortunately, this isn't always how God operates. If we want to follow him, we must be willing to deviate from our plans and remain open to what he is doing. This might mean practicing hospitality when we don't want to or helping others when it is inconvenient.

Are you open to unplanned encounters with others? Or do you hold stubbornly to your plans and schedules? Remember that God won't typically operate on your terms. Being involved in the work of the Father often means letting go of control and being flexible enough to be led by the Holy Spirit. Ask God to give you an awareness of what he is doing so that your heart can remain soft.

Father, help me see people as you do. May I welcome everyone you send my way.

HARD WORK

The lazy will not get what they want,
but those who work hard will.

PROVERBS 13:4 NCV

The Bible is straightforward about how we are to view hard work. God encourages us to have a strong work ethic. When we work hard, we are not idle. When we work hard, we enjoy the benefits of a job well done. When we work hard, we embrace displaying godly character for all who see us. We will not be left wanting after a lifetime of doing our best. Instead, God promises that he will reward us.

Are you embracing what it means to work hard in your season of life? Ask God to show you what doing your best looks like right now. Then, be quick to listen to what he says. Allow him to direct your life and seek to honor the way that he leads you. Seek to serve God with all your might, no matter what it looks like.

Father, help me be a hard worker for you. Show me what it looks like to work hard in this season of my life.

JUNE

Gray hair is a crown of splendor;
it is attained in the way of righteousness.

Proverbs 16:31 NIV

STEADY AND SATISFIED

Keep your lives free from the love of money and be content with what you have, because God has said, "Never will I leave you; never will I forsake you."

HEBREWS 13:5 NIV

It's easy to be mesmerized by online offers flashing in front of our eyes. We might visualize ourselves in that new dress or behind the wheel of that new car. We are enticed even though we have a full closet and a perfectly good vehicle. Why do we perpetually want more? Nothing will ever satisfy us more than the love of God and salvation through the blood of Christ.

As a grandparent, you get to choose what kind of life you will model for your grandchildren. Will they look back and remember that you were content, peaceful, and satisfied with all that God has given you? Or will they look back and remember your stories of frustration and what ifs? Will they remember you as disgruntled or calm and steady? This is a choice that only you can make.

Father, help me to display thankfulness for all that you've given me.

NOW AND FOREVER

Jesus Christ is the same yesterday and today and forever.

Hebrews 13:8 NIV

Is there anything in this life that we can count on to stay the same? We know that nothing is constant. Relationships change and evolve, the culture continuously shifts, and the economy ebbs and flows. Everything that this world has to offer is temporary and fleeting. The only thing that is truly reliable is Jesus. He will never change. For all eternity, his promises will remain. His character will not evolve or deteriorate. Everything about him will stay the same.

You might feel like you can't keep up with all the changes in your life. Babies are being born, children are graduating college or getting married, and people are retiring left and right. It's a busy and full season of life. All the while, you're dealing with your own feelings about aging. No matter how tumultuous things may feel, Christ is steady. He cannot be moved or shaken. He remains strong during life's fiercest storms and most gruesome battles.

Jesus, thank you for your consistency and unchanging presence in my life.

UNDENIABLE TRUTH

Do not be carried away by all kinds of strange teachings.

HEBREWS 13:9 NIV

As we watch people in the church deconstruct their faith, we know that we must be firmly committed to knowing and speaking God's truth. Our world has gone haywire, and evil is rampant. So many believers are walking away from God based on teaching that isn't biblical. We must be diligent and brave. We must persevere through difficult times so that we will be counted as faithful.

Let your grandchildren be blessed by seeing how fierce your faith is. Let them know that you are unwavering in your beliefs even when they are challenged by the world. As they see you remain strong in the face of adversity, they will learn two important truths. They will see that it is possible and attainable to be faithful to truth. They will also see the blessing that comes from persevering through difficulty.

God, help me defend your Word and speak its truth to my grandchildren.

SERVE WELL

"I have given you an example, that you also should do just as I have done to you."

John 13:15 ESV

Can you imagine the gasps around the room when Jesus offered to wash the disciple's feet? Here was their Lord, humbling himself to serve them in a lowly way. As Jesus washed their feet, he showed them what it looks like to love others. He also gave them a glimpse of the eternal sacrifice that he would later make.

Having already raised your children, you are familiar with what it looks like to sacrifice your time, energy, and resources for the good of someone else. You poured your life into your kids and now get to watch them do the same. As a grandmother, your directive is still to serve well and with humility. You might not be the one staying awake for endless hours with crying babies, but you can still lay your life down for your family.

Jesus, please give me a servant's heart like yours.
I want to serve my family well.

HONOR LEADERS

Have confidence in your leaders and submit to their authority, because they keep watch over you as those who must give an account. Do this so that their work will be a joy, not a burden, for that would be of no benefit to you.

HEBREWS 13:17 NIV

There is a burden that comes with leadership. The task of caring for other people is serious and weighty. With it comes a higher level of responsibility not to mention the drain it can be on emotions and mental capacity. Think of our pastors and their teams, do our actions consistently communicate that we understand and respect their position?

It's good to thank your leaders but it's more important to live in a way that honors their leadership and conveys that you trust their ability. To do this well, you must embrace humility. In a world that values self-escalation, it is refreshing and delightful to come across people who are confident enough to be respectful of leaders.

Father, help me to honor my leaders no matter my age.

MERCY AND DEED

Pray for us. We are sure that we have a clear conscience and desire to live honorably in every way.

HEBREWS 13:18 NIV

As Christians, we commit to a consistent relationship with Jesus. This means that we experience his love and mercy daily. It also means that we should daily desire to have a clear conscience and to live honorably. We often see Christians picking one of those things. They might focus entirely on the merciful love of Christ, giving themselves freedom to behave however they want. The other option is getting too caught up in rules and restrictions to please God. It's important that we embrace both aspects of Christianity.

As they learn how to walk with Jesus, remember to pray for this type of balance in your grandchildren's lives. Ask God that they would grasp the depth of his love and that as a result they would live in a God-fearing way. Seek to display the beauty of both things in your own life.

Father, help me experience your love in such a way that it changes how I live.

GOOD FRIENDS

Spend time with the wise and you will become wise,
but the friends of fools will suffer.

PROVERBS 13:20 NCV

At this point in our lives, we've seen the impact that other people can have on us. We know that bad company corrupts good character, and we are experienced enough to know we aren't immune to the influences of others. This isn't usually the case for our grandchildren. Early in life the desire for acceptance can often be greater than the ability to choose good friends. As grandparents we can help the children in our life make wise choices that will have a positive impact for years to come.

You might not be observing your grandkids daily interactions with their friends, but you do have the ability to pray and intercede for them. Ask God to give them wisdom and a soft heart. When you can, ask them questions about the relationships in their life. Keep communication open and consistent by showing that you have the humility to listen and the wisdom to ask good questions.

Jesus, give my grandchildren the wisdom and discernment to choose good friends.

HANDLING FEAR

"Do not let your hearts be troubled."

JOHN 14:1 NIV

No matter the reason, when our grandchild is afraid, we have an opportunity to speak God's truth to them. We can hold them close and tell them not to be afraid. We can share the truth of scripture and remind them what God says about our fear. We can pray over them and ask God to fill their hearts with truth. We can show them how to take their fears and surrender them to God.

How do you handle your grandchildren's fear? Do you brush it off or do you grasp ahold of the chance to reflect God's character? If you pay attention, each interaction you have with them can be a chance to teach them about who God is. Your reaction to their big emotions can speak volumes. As you approach their emotions in a godly way, it can equip them to handle themselves in a healthy way for the rest of their lives.

Father, help me to teach my grandchildren how to handle fear in a healthy way.

HOME FOR ETERNITY

"In my Father's house are many mansions; if it were not so, I would have told you. I go to prepare a place for you."

JOHN 14:2 NKJV

Many of us have never wondered where we will sleep at night. We are blessed to have a bed in a comfortable home. If God has provided for us in this lifetime, how much more will he do so for eternity? Jesus assures us that our heavenly home is already being prepared for us. God, who weaves together every detail of the universe, is creating a place for us to be with him forever. There is no perfection on this earth that compares to what we will experience on that great day.

Do thoughts of your heavenly home fill you with anticipation? The perfection that is promised should give you hope and allow you to persevere whatever trial is thrown your way. When you keep your eyes focused on what's to come, the troubles of the world don't seem quite as daunting. Whether you are facing health problems or relationship strife, there is perfection waiting for you.

Jesus, thank you for the glorious home you have prepared for me.

YOUTHFUL DEVOTION

You are my hope;
LORD God, You are my confidence from my youth.

PSALM 71:5 NASB

Some of us have followed Jesus for many years. We grew up in Christian homes and have done our best to honor God most of our lives. Some of us turned to God at a later age and don't have those early years of devotion to look back on. We didn't spend our youth using God as a compass to make wise decisions. We might even wish that someone had been there to guide us amid our struggles.

Imagine if your grandchildren grew up with a confident belief in God. Imagine if they understood his character rightly and didn't spend years questioning his existence or devotion to them. As their grandmother, you can pass the truth down to them. No matter what your own testimony is, you can teach them about who God is and essentially give them a head start. Ask God to draw them to himself at a young age.

Father, help my grandchildren's youth be defined by devotion to you.

BUILD UP

Let us aim for harmony in the church
and try to build each other up.

Romans 14:19 NLT

Far too many unnecessary offenses and petty disagreements have broken up relationships. The enemy loves to see God's children at odds, sacrificing unity in exchange for arguments and frustration. To honor God, we should care for each other and put each other's needs above our own. We must remember that as the Body of Christ, we are all on the same team. We must follow the commands of Christ to love God above all else and to love each other as he has loved us.

Sometimes unity in the Body of Christ can feel conceptual and not very practical. Remember that every interaction you have with a believer is an interaction with the Body. This means that if they are believers, the way you interact with your children and grandchildren falls into that directive. As such, scripture tells you to aim for harmony and build each other up.

Jesus, help me to honor you by building up my family.

GOOD FEAR

Those who fear the LORD are secure;
he will be a refuge for their children.

PROVERBS 14:26 NLT

Many people stumble over the command to fear the Lord until they understand the true meaning of the word. We are not to cower in fear of God, or tremble as we approach him. We are not supposed to view him as scary. The true definition of biblical fear is respect for God. We are to treat him with admiration and reverence. It is such a high level of respect that our behavior is changed because of it.

When you live your life in fear of God, those around you will notice. As you seek to respect and honor him in all that you do, others will take notice of his blessings in your life. Proverbs says that when you fear the Lord, he will be a refuge for your children. What a wonderful legacy to leave for your family!

Father, I want to honor and respect you in all that I do. I stand in reverence of who you are and all you do.

JUNE 13

"Peace I leave with you, My peace I give to you; not as the world gives do I give to you. Let not your heart be troubled, neither let it be afraid."

John 14:27 NKJV

We live in a world that lacks peace. If we look to our current society for serenity, we simply won't find it. Instead, we will be offered temporary satisfaction and half solutions. The comfort Jesus gives is counterculture. It's the only thing that reaches deep into our spirit and truly restores our soul.

Most believers go through a season when they are tempted by what the world has to offer. Your grandchildren will be no different. Remind them that Christ's peace is greater than anything they can conjure up on their own. His peace is all they need and all that will truly sustain them. Ask God to give them grace to accept his peace instead of the world's false satisfaction.

Jesus, keep my grandchildren in perfect peace, safe and secure in your arms.

ROOT OF ANGER

People with understanding control their anger;
a hot temper shows great foolishness.

PROVERBS 14:29 NLT

The root of anger is often pride or selfishness. We react negatively because at the core of the situation, we aren't getting what we want. We are inconvenienced, offended, or resentful and instead of surrendering our situation to God, we lash out in frustration. Proverbs reminds us that unleashing our temper proves to others that we are foolish. This type of behavior certainly won't display Christ's love to anyone.

You likely don't want to be considered foolish. If anger is causing you to lose control, repent and ask God for forgiveness. Do the hard work of unearthing your frustration and be consistent in bringing it to God. Let the Holy Spirit do a transformative work in your heart. He will be faithful to help you when you go to him in humility.

Father, please forgive me for my lack of self-control. In my anger, help me not to sin.

GENTLE ANSWERS

A gentle answer will calm a person's anger,
but an unkind answer will cause more anger.

PROVERBS 15:1 NCV

If you have ever been on the receiving end of an unkind word, you know how much it hurts—especially if it is undeserved. Children are particularly good at wielding harmful words. Arguments can easily escalate if they haven't yet learned how to have self-control. The immaturity and the lack of control over their words needs constant training and correction. They must be taught to speak lovingly, to show kindness, and to seek healing instead of destruction.

As a grandmother, you can share Christ's love by speaking to your grandchildren in a loving way. When they are unkind, correct them and encourage them. Your patience and gentleness can be a great example of the patience and gentleness that God also offers them. Your grandchildren probably won't remember the gifts you give them, but they will remember the way you made them feel. The words you use are a big part of that.

Father, please help me guard my tongue. I want my words to reflect your love.

UNUSED GIFTS

Everything that was written in the past was written to teach us. The Scriptures give us patience and encouragement so that we can have hope.

ROMANS 15:4 NCV

God spoke through man so that we can have his Word as our daily guide. Apart from the guidance of the Holy Spirit, it's our greatest asset as believers. If we don't utilize it, we are giving up a tool that is meant to improve our lives exponentially. It's a classic case of knowing what is right and continuing to make the wrong choice. Even with the Word readily available, many of us don't integrate it into our daily lives.

Have you developed the habit of saturating your life with the Word? Do you treat it as the gift that it is, or have you noticed yourself taking it for granted? No matter your age, it is never too late to incorporate new practices into your life. Try reading even one verse each day and ask the Holy Spirit to guide you and give you fresh eyes.

Jesus, thank you for the gift of your Word. Help me to see it and use it rightly.

ACCEPT OTHERS

Accept each other just as Christ has accepted you so that God will be given glory.

ROMANS 15:7 NLT

The Father does not play favorites. He is an equal opportunity God when it comes to offering salvation and sanctification. He says to come as we are, for he knows our human nature better than we do. We don't need to be perfect or have all our ducks in a row. In the same way, we should accept others. Our kindness shouldn't have limits or requirements. Instead, we are called to love others in the same extravagant and undeserved way that God love us.

If you are honest with yourself, do you show preference in the way that you love others? Ask the Holy Spirit to show you the state of your heart and trust his gentle leadership. He might show you that you are putting too much value on appearance, status, or wealth. If that's the case, have the humility to repent and ask for forgiveness.

Father, help me to never give preference to people for the way they look or their position in life. Help me love like you do.

CLEAR DIRECTIONS

Rejoice in hope, be patient in tribulation, be constant in prayer.

ROMANS 12:12 ESV

This passage in Romans provides such clear and concise direction. We can apply those three directives to any season of life. No matter what we are going through, we know that we will honor God if we obey this scripture. *Rejoice in hope, be patient in tribulation, be constant in prayer.* We can praise God because we know that he will accomplish his promises. We can be patient because we know that trials produce perseverance. We can be constant in prayer because we know that when we are in communion with God, we'll have his perspective on our situation.

There is nothing that you can face on this earth that God cannot guide you through. Maybe you are not the grandparent you wish you were. Maybe you live far from loved ones and are pained by your loneliness. Maybe your children aren't honoring the Lord, and it hurts your heart. No matter what type of trial you are experiencing, Scripture can be applied.

Lord, help me follow your scripture and do what you say.

TRUSTWORTHY

May the God of hope fill you with all joy and peace as you trust in him, so that you may overflow with hope by the power of the Holy Spirit.

ROMANS 15:13 NIV

At times God's plans for our lives might seem stalled, derailed, or even non-existent. We assume that he has turned a deaf ear, and we stop asking him for help. Those are the times he is working on our behalf in unseen ways and places. We don't serve a God who sits back and is uninvolved in our lives. God is never silent as we understand silence.

If you are feeling hopeless, or like you can't see God moving in your life, turn to Scripture. If you want to be filled with joy, peace, and hope, you need to trust in God. Trust that he keeps his promises. Trust that he will never forsake you. Trust that he has good things in store for you.

Father, I know that you are trustworthy. Help me to remember your promises and wait patiently for your promises to be fulfilled.

DILIGENT IN REPENTANCE

The LORD does not listen to the wicked,
but he hears the prayers of those who do right.

PROVERBS 15:29 NCV

When we choose to live in disobedience, we put distance between ourselves and God. If we continually engage in sin without repentance, we keep ourselves from being as close to God as we should be. We get to be as close to him as we want. If we seek him, we will find him. If we surrender our sins and trust in Christ's sacrifice on the cross, we will never be far from him.

The repentance of sin is not a popular topic in today's culture. It's common to hear that you can live however you want to, and still reap all the benefits that God has to offer. This simply isn't true. Pray for your grandchildren as this message surrounds them. Remind them that obedience is part of the package. We must turn from our sin if we want to experience God's grace.

Father, help me to be diligent in repenting from sin. I want my prayers to be heard.

JUNE 21

BAD COMPANY

Do not be deceived:
"Bad company ruins good morals."

1 CORINTHIANS 15:33 ESV

We will inevitably become like those who we spend the most time with. We've seen this play out in our children's lives, and we know that as our grandchildren get older, they too will have to make wise decisions about their friends. While it's easy to see this tendency in young people, we should also be aware of the impact of others on our adult friendships.

Be aware of how your friendships are affecting you. Even as adults we can sometimes desire to have companionship even if it's having a negative effect. Do your relationships push you closer to the Lord and encourage you to honor him? Ask the Holy Spirit for discernment and he will help you to navigate your relationships.

Father, help me choose likeminded friends. I want my closest friends to be a good influence on me.

HIS SALVATION

May the God of peace be with all of you.

ROMANS 15:33 CSB

In a world that severely lacks peace, we have the blessing of knowing exactly where to run when we are distraught. When everything around us seems tumultuous and we are overwhelmed by the worlds suffering, we find our refuge in God. He gives us peace that doesn't make sense, can't be duplicated anywhere else, and doesn't have limits.

Don't be dismayed by the state of the world. Don't be dismayed by conflict in your life or unexpected trials. You are a child of the God of peace. He longs to quiet your heart and fill you with peace. He doesn't want his children to be anxious, scared, or frustrated.

God, thank you for your great peace. Help me to run to you when I am overwhelmed.

POWERFUL SIMPLICITY

Flesh and blood cannot inherit the kingdom of God, nor does the perishable inherit the imperishable.

1 Corinthians 15:50 ESV

Many people miss the point of the gift of salvation because it just seems too easy. They can't get past the fact that someone would pay for their sins. They insist on having to do something as their part in the process. Our salvation is based on Jesus alone. Without the power of the cross we would be lost forever.

Today, remember the simple power of the gospel. Ask yourself if there is any area of your life where you are placing more value on your actions than on the sacrificial work of Jesus. A works mentality can pop up in small ways that you might not notice right away. Ask the Holy Spirit for discernment and trust his gracious leadership.

Jesus, thank you for your sacrifice which has saved me.

SERVE HIM

Be steadfast, immovable, always abounding in the work of the Lord, knowing that in the Lord your labor is not in vain.

1 CORINTHIANS 15:58 ESV

Our service to God should be unyielding, loyal, and abundant. This might seem like a daunting task. Instead of feeling discouraged by the idea of constant work, remember that when something is in alliance with God's will, he gives us the grace we need to accomplish it. Furthermore, he promises that nothing we do is in vain. We will all be compensated, and extravagantly rewarded for the work we do.

You can serve the Lord for all your days, no matter your age or physical condition. We are called to be steadfast in our service. Ask God how you can best serve him in this season of your life. He will speak clearly when you ask him for help.

Father, help me to be faithful in serving you.

THE SAME POWER

Commit your actions to the LORD,
and your plans will succeed.

PROVERBS 16:3 NLT

Wouldn't we love a guarantee that our life's efforts will always be successful? If we trust in our own abilities and do things our own ways, we are not guaranteed that it will be fruitful. Scripture says that if we commit our plans to God, we will succeed. We can do nothing without him, but with him mountains can move.

With God's strength there is nothing that can't be achieved. The supernatural power that lives in us is the same power that raised Jesus from the grave. When you commit your plans to God, you acknowledge that you need his help and that his ways are higher than your own.

Father, I commit this day to you. Lead me where you want me to go.

GOOD NEWS

"Go into all the world and preach the Good News to everyone."

MARK 16:15 NLT

The command to make disciples is applicable to all of us. Sometimes we compartmentalize this verse and assume that it's meant for missionaries. The truth that all of us are capable of sharing the gospel. We can display Christ's love to our family, our friends, our neighbors, and our coworkers.

If you ask God for opportunities to share the gospel, he will give them to you. He loves it when his children find freedom through the cross. His desire is that everyone would be saved, and you can partner with him to accomplish that goal. You can speak truth when the opportunity arises, and you can teach others about the character of God through your actions.

God, I want to partner with you in your work. Help me to be aware of opportunities to share truth and give me the courage to speak up.

FALSE PROPHETS

Watch out for people who cause divisions and upset people's faith by teaching things contrary to what you have been taught. Stay away from them.

ROMANS 16:17 NLT

The Bible warns us about false prophets. Many will say they serve Christ, but their lives aren't surrender to him and they don't live in obedience to God's Word. As believers, we must be wary of false teachings and use discernment in what we allow to influence us. The best way to stay on the narrow path is to be familiar with the truth. The more we study the Word, the quicker we will recognize false teaching.

Don't be nervous about false teaching. You don't have to be afraid that you'll go astray or that you'll wander out of God's will. As you familiarize yourself with the Word, it should give you confidence and a sense of security. There is nothing to fear when God is on your side.

Jesus, give me wisdom to know when someone is a false prophet. I want to stay faithful to the truth.

WARY OF PRIDE

Pride comes before destruction,
and an arrogant spirit before a fall.

PROVERBS 16:18 CSB

We often attribute stubbornness and immaturity to children. Truly, there is little difference between the stubbornness of a child and an adult. Both are declaring that they can accomplish something within their own abilities, not needing or wanting help from anyone else. This type of pride always ends in destruction.

When the children in your life are prideful, their destruction usually comes in the form of losing a privilege or dealing with the discipline of the parents. When you, as an adult, engage in pride, the consequences are much greater. You risk damaging your relationships, losing favor at your workplace, and putting distance between you and God. Be wary of pride. Ask God to keep your heart soft and engaged in humility.

God, help me to embrace humility. I don't want to deal with prides destruction in my life.

GOOD GRAYS

Gray hair is like a crown of honor;
it is earned by living a good life.

PROVERBS 16:31 NCV

It is a privilege to get older. Our culture often scorns the aging process, but the truth is that it is a great blessing to be alive. Gray hair should be seen as a beautiful accomplishment. No matter what the beauty standards of the world are, gray hair should be praised. It shows that a life has been well lived.

No matter how you feel about gray hair on a superficial level, know in your heart that it is a crown of glory. Each day that you have lived is a testament to your creator. The longevity of your life shows his faithfulness and his great care for you. Each gray hair is evidence that God has sustained you and watched over you all your days.

Father, thank you for your faithfulness in my life. Help me not to scorn the aging process but to delight in you instead.

DIFFERENT REALITY

"If you have faith as small as a mustard seed, you can say to this mulberry tree, 'Be uprooted and planted in the sea,' and it will obey you."

LUKE 17:6 NIV

Our grandchildren are enthralled when they role-play. They envision being mighty warriors or princesses in a tower. They can dive into the story with their hearts, minds, and emotions. They can't see dragons or great battles, but they behave as if they can. This is a great picture of what our faith is meant to look like. Even when we can't see what God is doing, our belief in him affects every aspect of our life. Our reality looks different from those who don't follow God.

Faith is not something that you muster up. If you are discouraged by your lack of faith, don't despair. As you surrender to the Lord, ask him for help and he will strengthen your faith. He will bolster your belief and make you stronger. He is fully capable of doing a miracle in your life and will increase your faith if you ask.

Jesus, I believe. Please give me great faith. I want my belief in you to impact every area of my life.

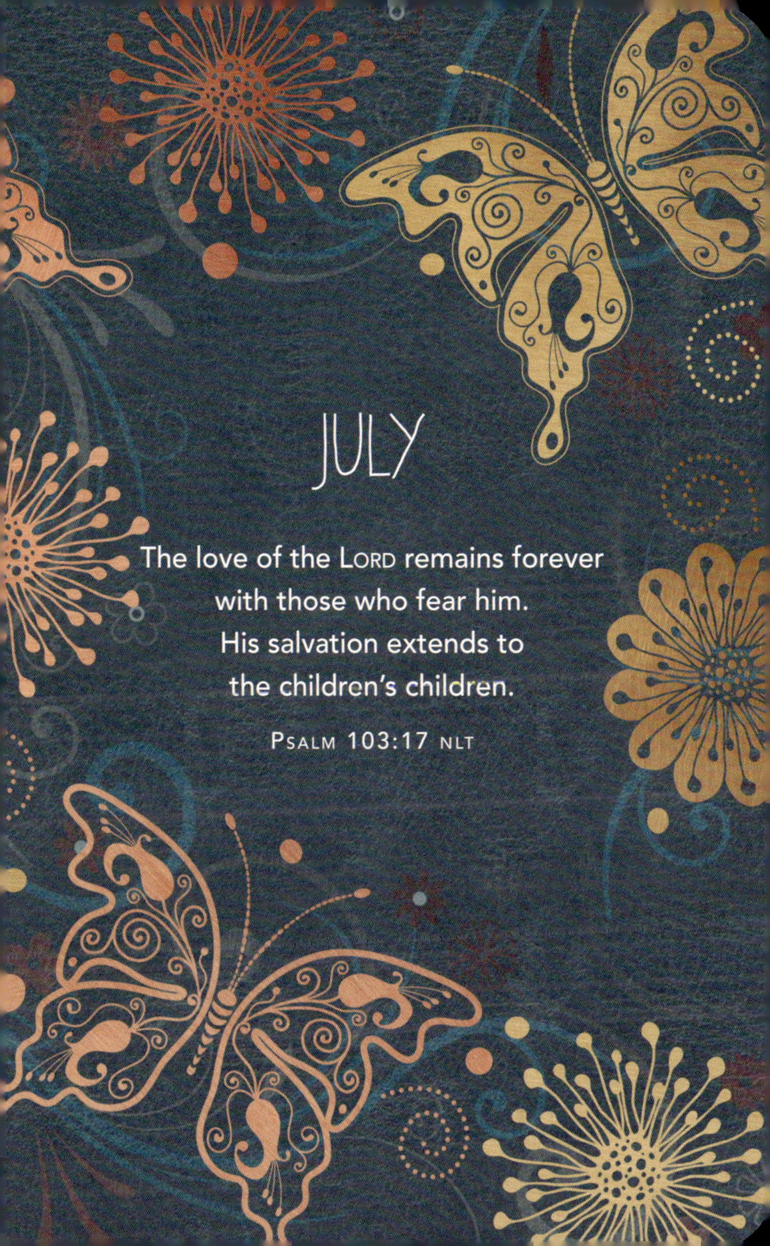
JULY
The love of the LORD remains forever
with those who fear him.
His salvation extends to
the children's children.
PSALM 103:17 NLT

AMAZING BLESSING

Grandchildren are the crowning glory of the aged;
parents are the pride of their children.

PROVERBS 17:6 NLT

Don't we all light up when we see our grandchild running toward us? It is such a great feeling to scoop them up in our arms. Our phones are filled with precious pictures that we happily share with anyone at any time. Families are one of God's greatest blessings. They are evidence of his loving desire to give us good gifts.

Today, thank God for the gift of your family. Each member of your family is a precious creation. This is a wonderful season of your life. Thank God for the way that he has grown your family and take a moment to revel in the beauty of it. Five, ten, or fifteen years ago you probably wondered what this season would look like, and now you're in it.

Father, thank you for the incredible blessing of grandchildren!

CLOSER THAN BROTHERS

A friend is always loyal,
and a brother is born to help in time of need.

PROVERBS 17:17 NLT

A true friend doesn't come and go based on how easy your relationship is. A true friend stays close, even when trials arise, and the road gets rocky. Difficult seasons have a way of revealing the loyalty of those around us. When someone is faithful through suffering, that should be counted as a great blessing.

Today, thank God for the people in your life who have been loyal and committed. It's a delight to be able to share life's highs and lows with someone you can trust. Tell your friends what a gift they are. If you're in a season of loneliness, ask God a friend. He cares about your heart, and he cares about your relationships.

Father, please help me choose my friends wisely. I want to enjoy the loyalty of a kind and godly friend.

TRUE HAPPINESS

A happy heart is like good medicine,
but a broken spirit drains your strength.

PROVERBS 17:22 NCV

The world will tell us that the most important thing is to follow our happiness wherever it might lead us. As Christians, we know that this is not how we are supposed to live. We've been called to surrender at the cross and follow Jesus wherever he might lead us. However, it is important to remember that your happiness is not unnoticed by God. He is not a tyrant, demanding that we all solemnly follow him to our own detriment.

As a child of God, your happiness matters to him. He doesn't want you to walk through your life with a crushed spirit and a downcast attitude. His desire is for you to live abundantly and full of joy. As you spend time in his presence, ask God how you can have more joy in your life. Trust that he sees you and has good things in store for you.

Father, thank you for the true joy that comes from you. Fill my heart with gladness as I follow you.

STRONG AND STEADY

The LORD is my rock, my protection, my Savior.
My God is my rock.
I can run to him for safety.
He is my shield and my saving strength, my defender.

PSALM 18:2 NCV

In this season of life, we may face trouble that we are unfamiliar with. As our children grow and potentially marry, we are navigating having new members of our family. As grandchildren enter the world, we are learning how to support our children as they learn to parent for the first time. As we get older, we are dealing with the challenges that come with aging. No matter what we face, God is steady and unchanging.

God is your rock, your shield, and your defender. He knows exactly what you need and will protect you in times of trouble. You can rely on him because he is trustworthy and strong. He has proven himself time and time again. When you run to him, he will not fail you. No matter how foreign this season feels, God is your saving strength.

Father, help me to run to you when I am overwhelmed.

CHERISH THEM

"If anyone causes one of these little ones—those who believe in me—to stumble, it would be better for them to have a large millstone hung around their neck and to be drowned in the depths of the sea."

MATTHEW 18:6 NIV

God is fiercely protective of children. He loves them dearly and expects us to care for them well. When we are in the position to influence children, we should take our role very seriously. It's a privilege to help shape the life of another person. When we care for children with patience and kindness, we display God's love for them.

As a grandmother, you have endless opportunities to cherish and protect your grandchildren. They are precious in God's eyes and should be treated as such. Every child is valuable and worthy of extravagant love. Shower them with affection and be a steady presence of wisdom in their lives.

Father, help me to love the children in my life like you do. I want to take my role seriously and do it well.

GATHER TOGETHER

"Where two or three are gathered together in my name, I am there in the midst of them."

MATTHEW 18:20 NKJV

When we gather in his name, God is with us. If Scripture says that he will be there, then we can trust that he will keep his promise. We can have faith in him and trust that we are never out of his sight nor his hearing. There is power in numbers when it comes to prayer.

If you are discouraged or are facing a trial, remember the value of gathering in prayer. Call a few friends and ask them to sit and pray with you. You are not meant to figure everything out on your own. God knows that we need each other. He designed us to thrive in community, consistently relying on each other to stay on the narrow path. Don't forsake meeting with believers to pray. It will strengthen your faith and your relationships with each other.

Jesus, thank you for hearing us when we pray together. Help me to remember the power of gathering in your name.

TAKE INVENTORY

Keep cleansing me, God,
and keep me from my secret, selfish sins;
may they never rule over me!
For only then will I be free from fault
and remain innocent of rebellion.

PSALM 19:13 TPT

When we ask God to refine us, it requires us to periodically take inventory of our thoughts and actions. The more we learn about what is pleasing to God, the more we can shape our lives to honor him. We are all prone to different sins and the process of sanctification will look different for everyone. No matter what your journey looks like, keep God at the center.

As you seek to honor the Lord, continue asking him for help. He will show you the areas of your life that need attention. He is a gentle and kind teacher who always wants what is best for you. Keep your heart soft to conviction and follow God's leadership.

God, I surrender my life to you. Show me where I have sin take root in my life. Help me to honor you in all that I do.

LOVE THE LOWLY

"Let the little children come to me, and do not hinder them, for the kingdom of heaven belongs to such as these."

MATTHEW 19:14 NIV

While on earth, Jesus welcomed children. He didn't care that everyone else thought they were inconvenient or not worth his time. Often, our idea of what is important is completely different from God's. His kingdom challenges our priorities and preconceived notions of what status looks like. Welcoming children was just one way that God emphasized that he will always prioritize the lowly and forgotten.

If God showered love and affection on the lowly, then you should too. Without the influence of God, your ideas of status, success, or importance are likely wrong. Embrace God's upside-down kingdom and remember that he elevated those that the world didn't think were worthy.

God, I know that you see the lowly and forgotten. Help me to love those that the world doesn't consider worthy of love.

THOUGHTS AND WORDS

Let the words of my mouth
and the meditation of my heart
be acceptable in your sight,
O Lord, my rock and my redeemer.

Psalm 19:14 ESV

Typically, the Christian community is more concerned with the words we say than the meditations of our hearts. Scripture outlines that both are important and should be paid attention to. We can't just seek to control our tongues while our minds are filled with negativity or even wicked thoughts. Both our words and our thoughts should be acceptable to God.

If you find yourself thinking things you would never say out loud perhaps you've let your thought life become undisciplined. The good news is that you are always able to grow and change. Ask God for help and he will be faithful to teach and guide you. He knows what is best for you and he wants you to have a healthy thought life. This isn't simply because he says so, but because he knows that you will have a more abundant and joyous life when you are thinking rightly.

Father, I want to honor you with my thoughts and words. Help me to pay attention to both.

ACCEPT CORRECTION

Listen to advice and accept correction,
and in the end you will be wise.

PROVERBS 19:20 NCV

We've all observed a child whose parents let them run wild. There is often a lack of boundaries and little correction. Disciplining with kindness and love sets children up for success later in life. They will learn what is right and wrong as well as how to make wise decisions. Even as adults, we must be open to the correction of others.

As you raised your children, and now as you're involved with grandchildren, you're likely very familiar with what it looks like to correct naughty behavior. Remember that you are also in need of kind and loving corrections. Put people in your life who seek godly wisdom and can hold you accountable. Trust their opinions and seek to follow the Holy Spirit.

Father, please do what is necessary to make me more like Jesus. Help me to be open to the correction of others.

GOOD PLANS

You can make many plans,
but the LORD's purpose will prevail.

PROVERBS 19:21 NLT

No matter how thoroughly we plan or how hard we work, our plans don't matter if they don't align with God's. When we follow him, we realize that his ideas are always best. The idea that God will only ask us to do things we don't want to do is wrong. He knows us perfectly and we are most fulfilled when we operate in the way that he designed for us.

God's plans for you are not a mystery. They are not a trap meant to beat you into holy submission. God's plans are full of freedom and grace. He knows what is best for you and will faithfully lead you toward an abundant life that is filled with the fruit of the spirit.

Father, thank you for your good plans. Help me to trust your ideas and lean on you for guidance.

TRUST IN GOD

Some trust in chariots and some in horses,
but we trust in the name of the LORD our God.

PSALM 20:7 NIV

It's easy to say that we trust in God but does our reality line up with our words? We cannot be actively trusting God while still panicking when our plans change, or we lose control of a situation. Sometimes, when trials arise, we realize that our trust has been in our ability to manage our lives. When the unexpected happens, we quickly see where our allegiance lies.

Scripture reminds us not to depend on ourselves or to rely on our own understanding. We are to acknowledge God and bring him into every detail of our lives. Especially when we are comfortable and unbothered, we should ask God to renew our trust in his faithfulness.

Thank you, Father, for being so good and trustworthy. I want to rely on you not on my own strength.

BEWARE OF SOME

"Beware of the teachers of the law. They like to walk around in flowing robes and love to be greeted with respect in the marketplaces and have the most important seats in the synagogues and the places of honor at banquets. They devour widows' houses and for a show make lengthy prayers."

LUKE 20:46-47 NIV

The world is full of people who claim to know that truth but aren't following God. This is why it's important that we use discernment when it comes to who we listen to. We shouldn't be swayed by the loudest, most passionate, or most popular opinion. Instead, we should devote ourselves to the consistent study of God's Word.

As you hide Scripture in your heart, you'll be less easily swayed by lies. As such, you can help your children and grandchildren do the same. You have a lifetime of reading the Word under your belt. Pray for wisdom for your family and when the opportunity arises, teach them about what God says.

Father, help me to stay aware of false teachers. I don't want to be swayed by popular opinions.

COMPLETE RESPECT

LORD, teach me what you want me to do,
and I will live by your truth.
Teach me to respect you completely.

PSALM 86:11 NCV

What does it look like to show someone respect? If we respect someone, we will listen when they speak, we will take notice of their good qualities, and we will trust their competency. These are all ways that we can display respect for God. We can stay attuned to his voice, we can pay attention to his good works, and we can trust that he is able to do everything he says he will.

You've probably told your children, and now your grandchildren, to respect their parents or other authority figures in their lives. Ideally, your admonition to them should be reflected by your sincere respect of God. Today, ask yourself if you are completely respectful of your creator.

Father, thank you for who you are and all you've done. I want to respect you completely.

SOMEPLACE BETTER

"He will wipe every tear from their eyes, and there will be no more death or sorrow or crying or pain. All these things are gone forever."

REVELATION 21:4 NLT

Jesus said we would have trouble in this world because we were not made for this world. We were made for someplace better—the kingdom of God. While we live on earth, we encounter sorrow, joy, success, and failure, all mingled together. We don't have a concept for what it's like to experience zero pain or difficulty. We're so used to the suffering of this life that we cannot comprehend what is to come.

The suffering that you experience will not last forever! Better days are coming. You were intended to live in perfection. When Jesus comes back and makes all things right, we will experience life as it was meant to be. Let the anticipation of that day strengthen your faith and fill you with hope.

Jesus, I cannot wait to spend eternity with you! Fill me with the hope of your return.

ANXIETIES OF LIFE

"Be careful, or your hearts will be weighed down with carousing, drunkenness and the anxieties of life, and that day will close on you suddenly like a trap."

LUKE 21:34 NIV

While several texts focus on the sin of drunkenness, we should be careful to read the entirety of this scripture. God includes carousing and being weighed down with anxiety in the same list. None of these things reflect God's best for us. When we allow anxiety to rule our lives, we dwell on fear and ruminate on problems that might not even exist. This is not indicative of the abundant life that God desires for his children.

If you find yourself constantly worried, ask God to guide your thoughts. It might take hard work, but you can change the way that you think. Fill your mind with truth and continuously cast your anxious thoughts upon the Lord. He is well equipped to deal with them and in exchange he will give you peace.

Father, protect me from anxiety. May my thoughts be filled with truth instead of worry.

DRAW THEM

Train up a child in the way he should go;
even when he is old he will not depart from it.

PROVERBS 22:6 ESV

It's likely that most of us have adult children who are not following the Lord. Statistically, some of our children may have seasons where they reject the truth and choose a different path. This can be painful and difficult to watch. We wonder if we did something wrong and worry that they won't return to the Lord.

If this is part of your story, let the God of all peace comfort you. He sees your grief and he knows how hurt you are. Ask for wisdom and discernment so that you might love your adult children well even when they aren't following the Lord. Intercede on their behalf and pray that God will draw them close.

Father, you know my heart breaks when my children don't follow you. Draw them close to you and in kindness lead them to repentance.

GOOD SHEPHERD

The LORD is my shepherd;
I have everything I need.

PSALM 23:1 NCV

When we follow our good shepherd, we have everything we need. We know that he will provide for us and take care of us well. We don't have to worry because our shepherd is capable, strong, and loving. We can rest and be at peace because there is nothing that can remove us from the presence of our great protector.

When you are tempted to worry, look to your shepherd. When you start to feel like you don't have what you need, ask God to remind you of his faithfulness. As you turn to him, your confidence will grow, and you will rely on truth instead of your feelings.

Father, help me to trust in you as my good shepherd. You say that I have all I need, and I want to trust in you.

GOOD CHARACTER

Even when I walk
through the darkest valley,
I will not be afraid,
for you are close beside me.
Your rod and your staff
protect and comfort me.

PSALM 23:4 NLT

It's easy to fret and worry when we are surrounded by darkness. It's important to remember that God is our protector in both literal and figurative darkness. No matter what trial we are facing, he promises to be nearby. It's his great kindness and consistent presence that causes us to be devoted to him.

Teach your grandchildren about how God is your good shepherd. Share with them how he leads us, protects us, and comforts us. It would be so wonderful if they grew up with an understanding not just of what God requires but of his character. It's easy to get caught up in correcting behaviors but try to spend an equal amount of time teaching your grandchildren about God's goodness and faithfulness.

Father, thank you for leading me with kindness.

COUNT THE COST

Surely goodness and mercy shall follow me
all the days of my life,
and I shall dwell in the house of the LORD forever.

PSALM 23:6 ESV

When we choose to follow Jesus we surrender our plans, our ambitions, and our earthly satisfaction. If our faith is going to have longevity, we must remember the wildly good things that God gives us. He promises that goodness and mercy will follow us. He offers an eternity of joy in his presence and a place to sit at his table. His gifts are worth far more than anything that we are giving up.

Each believer must count the cost of their salvation. Your children and grandchildren might be in that season right now. Don't be intimidated by their questions and frustrations. Their choice to follow God must come from a sincere heart. Pray that they will see the goodness that God offers and that they will be confident in their decision to follow him.

Father, give each member of my family a clear picture of what you offer. Help them to count the cost and then confidently choose you.

REMEMBER THEM

Listen to your father, who gave you life,
and do not forget your mother when she is old.

PROVERBS 23:22 NCV

We instruct our children and grandchildren to show respect when they are small, but it should not stop in childhood. We, ourselves, need to show our own parents respect if they are still with us. Just because we are grown adults does not mean that we are exempt from this portion of Scripture. Our actions toward our elderly parents should be patient, kind, and loving. We honor God when we remember our parents in their old age.

Maintaining healthy relationships with aging parents is not always easy. Especially if you are in the position of managing their healthcare, you may be tired and overwhelmed. Let God comfort you as you navigate this season of life. It's brand new for both of you and no one expects you to have it all figured out. Take a deep breath and ask God to give you perseverance.

Father, help me honor and love my parents. I want my actions to be pleasing to you.

ENDURE

"The one who endures to the end will be saved."

MATTHEW 24:13 NLT

The Christian walk is not a race that follows typical rules. There is not a singular winner, and our time doesn't mean anything. The only requirement is that we finish. If we don't quit, we win. All that is required of us is that we faithfully follow Jesus, keeping our faith steady until his return. The longevity of our faith matters far more than our own perceptions of success.

When you think about discipling or equipping your grandchildren remember that you want them to have a faith that lasts. Nothing matters more than having the ability to hang on. Trials, suffering, and failures will fade away when the end goal is simply to remain faithful to Jesus. Pray that above all else, perseverance would be prevalent in your grandchildren's lives.

Father, may I never fall away. Keep me on the narrow road and give my family perseverance to love you until you come back.

NO FEAR

"You also must be ready, for the Son of Man is coming at an hour you do not expect."

MATTHEW 24:44 ESV

God's Word says that Jesus will come like a thief in the night. The time and hour will not be known by anyone except God. On that day, we hope to be found faithfully waiting. We want to see him and rejoice. It would be awful to see him and be filled with shame or regret.

As you wait for Christ's return, remember that you are not supposed to wait in fear. God's kindness, not fear, is what draws you to true repentance. As you continuously follow him, leaning on his strength and casting your cares upon him, you have nothing to worry about. You are not waiting to be ambushed and judged. You are waiting for a face-to-face visit from your closest friend and your precious savior.

Jesus, help me to wait for you with anticipation and joy.

SMALL INCREMENTS

"Well done, my good and faithful servant. You have been faithful in handling this small amount, so now I will give you many more responsibilities. Let's celebrate together!"

Matthew 25:23 NLT

As we raised our children, we didn't wake up one day expecting our toddler to behave like a teenager. Instead, we gave them more responsibility in whatever increments they could handle. We watched them grow and be able to handle more each year. Slow growth ensures success and longevity.

The same thing is true with your relationship with God. As you grow and are faithful, God will give you more responsibility. He doesn't ask you to do things that you aren't equipped to do. Instead, he faithfully leads each of his children, giving them what is best for them. If you are in a season of waiting, trust that maybe God simply hasn't finished teaching you something yet.

Father, help me faithfully finish each task you give me. I don't want to rush your teaching.

SELF-CONTROL

If you live without restraint
and are unable to control your temper,
you're as helpless as a city with broken-down
defenses, open to attack.

PROVERBS 25:28 TPT

When our grandchildren throw temper tantrums, we are quick to correct them. We are quick to notice when children's emotions overflow. We know that they need to learn how to handle their emotions. We want to see them succeed in life and we know that self-control is needed.

There is nothing wrong with correcting a child, but you should also be aware of how you handle your own emotions. Do you display restraint and control your own temper? If the answer is no, it's time to do some hard work. Ask the Holy Spirit to soften your heart and teach you how to be healthy in this area of your life.

Father, I want to be self-controlled! Help me to manage my emotions in a healthy way.

DON'T HIDE

I do not spend time with liars,
nor do I make friends with those who hide their sin.

Psalm 26:4 NCV

We aren't supposed to be friends with people who hide their sins. This would imply that we should regularly be discussing and confessing our sins to each other. Otherwise, how would we know if someone is hiding sin? Honest and open conversations should be a normal occurrence in our friendships. When we are willing to easily share our shortcomings, we open the door for others to share as well.

If you've ever shared a mistake with someone, you might have noticed that your vulnerability led to them also speaking openly about sin. When you speak honestly, you remove the stigma and shame that sin can create. Instead of hiding in embarrassment, we make room for Christ's light to shine and bring freedom.

Father, please keep me closest with those who love you most.

CARRIED THROUGH

The LORD is my light and the one who saves me.
So why should I fear anyone?
The LORD protects my life.
So why should I be afraid?

PSALM 27:1 NCV

With God as our protector, we don't have to be afraid. There is nothing that people can do to us that can remove us from his presence. He is always with us, and he never forsakes us. When fear begins to creep in, we can lean on his strength and remember his great faithfulness.

As your grandchildren grow, every new thing they experience can seem scary. From their first day of kindergarten, to their first day at a new job, the young life is filled with potentially nerve-wracking firsts. As they grow, remind them of God's faithfulness. You have already done all those things, and you know that God carried you through. No matter what they are facing God is with them.

Father, thank you for being with me every second of my life. Help me to teach my grandchildren about your faithfulness.

LOVING CORRECTION

Wounds from a sincere friend
are better than many kisses from an enemy.

PROVERBS 27:6 NLT

When God speaks through a well-meaning friend, we should listen. It is better to pay attention to correction than to be stuck in sin later. Instead of being offended, we should be thankful for the presence of a caring friend. It takes courage to lovingly point out a flaw and we should cherish the friend who does it well.

As much as you might not like correction, it is wise to embrace it. Tell your close friends that you are open to their opinions. As you lovingly point each other toward godliness, you reap the benefits of iron sharpening iron. Today, thank the Lord for the godly friendships in your life.

Jesus, I want to be soft hearted and open to correction. Thank you for the friends in my life who help me to honor you.

GOODNESS EVERYWHERE

I remain confident of this:
I will see the goodness of the LORD
in the land of the living.

PSALM 27:13 NIV

Whenever tragedy strikes, people often blame God. The world is quick to point fingers and question why a good God would let bad things happen. What's interesting is that while they have no problem throwing accusations, they don't seem to be willing to attribute any good things to him. His goodness is everywhere.

As you've matured in your faith, you've probably noticed that you are quicker notice God's blessings. You've learned to pay attention to the good things that he is doing. The more you follow him, the more you will see him at work for the good of those who love him.

God, thank you for the good things in my life. Help me to see what you are doing and all the ways you've blessed me.

WHILE WE WAIT

Wait patiently for the LORD.
Be brave and courageous.
Yes, wait patiently for the LORD.

PSALM 27:14 NLT

We've all seen a grandchild wait in agony for a treat after dinner. It's impossible to wait for something so delicious! They squirm, whine, and bounce around, desperate for the green flag to grab a treat from the plate. Waiting is hard work for children, but we know that they will feel better if they don't eat the cookie right away.

The same concept can be applied to your relationship with God. When you are waiting for something, it's important to trust that God knows best. He doesn't ask his children to wait for no reason. There is always a purpose, and we can be confident that his ways are higher than ours.

Thank you, Lord, for helping me to wait. Help me to be patient and to lean on your understanding over my own.

LOVING ACCOUNTABILITY

As iron sharpens iron,
So one person sharpens another.

Proverbs 27:17 NASB

As we follow God, we are not meant to walk alone. We need the support, encouragement, and wisdom of other believers. We were each made uniquely, and we reflect different aspects of God's character. As such, when we walk in unity, we display a full picture of who he is. We should value the opinions of others and be open to correction.

Do you challenge your friends, and do they challenge you? If the answer is no, ask God for wisdom in how to develop the habit of mutual accountability. There is great reward in lovingly pushing each other toward godliness.

Jesus, teach me how to challenge other believers in a loving way. At the same time, help me to receive correction from those who love me.

AUGUST

Teach the older women to live in a way that honors God. They must not slander others or be heavy drinkers. Instead, they should teach others what is good.

TITUS 2:3 NLT

SUPERNATURAL BODYGUARD

The Lord is my strength and my shield;
my heart trusts in him, and he helps me.
My heart leaps for joy,
and with my song I praise him.

Psalm 28:7 NIV

We rejoice in the truth that we have a supernatural bodyguard. He sees every detail of our lives, and he knows exactly how and when we need protection. There is no trouble or trial that surprises him or is beyond his ability. We can walk through our days with confidence and joy because we know that we are safely in his hands.

Just as God has been faithful to protect you, he will be faithful to protect your children and grandchildren. Prayerfully commit them into his hands and then let your heart be at peace, knowing full well that his strength is more than enough for them. When you are tempted to worry or panic about their wellbeing, let your faith be increased by intercession. He is in control and sees all their comings and goings.

Thank you, my Protector, for keeping my family safe.

EVERY OPPORTUNITY

"Go therefore and make disciples of all the nations, baptizing them in the name of the Father and of the Son and of the Holy Spirit."

MATTHEW 28:19 NKJV

As both parents and grandparents, we probably expect obedience from children. When we give instructions, we would like them to be followed. If we didn't care about the task or outcome, we wouldn't have asked. The same concept can be applied to scripture. God has given us, his children, a directive to go and make disciples. Do we take his instruction seriously?

Making disciples might feel like a daunting task but your life is full of opportunities to be obedient to God's call. It doesn't mean that you must travel across the ocean or jump into full time traditional ministry. As you teach your children what it looks like to live a life that honors God, you are making disciples. As you show your grandchildren what it looks like to have unwavering faith in the face of adversity, you are making disciples.

Jesus, open my eyes to even the smallest opportunity to teach others about you.

ALWAYS NEAR

"Teach them to obey everything that I have taught you, and I will be with you always, even until the end of this age."

MATTHEW 28:20 NCV

If we embraced the truth found in Scripture, our general perspective on life would change radically. Jesus promises that he is with us *always*, even until the end of the age. The Son of God, the one who died and rose again for our sins, never leaves our side. There isn't a single moment in which we are left alone or forsaken. He doesn't turn away when we fail, and he isn't blind to our darkness. Instead, he stays close and equips us in our time of need.

As someone who has years of life experience under their belt, would you say you have lived as though Christ is always with you? It is never too late to embrace this truth. No matter how old you are physically, your spirit can be renewed and transformed. Today, ask God to give you a revelation of Christ's presence in your life. Be encouraged by his closeness.

Jesus, help me to be aware of your nearness. Thank you for never leaving me.

TRUE PEACE

Fools give full vent to their rage,
but the wise bring calm in the end.

PROVERBS 29:11 NIV

It is unsettling to be around people who cannot handle their anger. This is evidence that they lack self-control. As a result, people may feel insecure or even unsafe around them. Alternatively, it's calming to be with someone who is steadfast regardless of their circumstances. Their peaceful demeanor has an impact on everyone they encounter. True peace can only come from Jesus. This is good news because it means that it's accessible to everyone!

Maybe you're not the peaceful, restful grandmother that you thought you would be. You want to bring calmness to those around you but maybe you're struggling to get there. Even if you feel like you are not a peaceful person, there is hope. True peace isn't something you are born with or can muster up on your own. Instead, it is a fruit of the spirit. As you submit to Christ and walk in his ways, you are promised to bear the fruit of peace.

Father, please fill me afresh with your Spirit. I want to experience your peace and pass it on to others.

SEEK

"You will seek me and find me,
when you seek me with all your heart."

JEREMIAH 29:13 ESV

We know what it's like to want something and work to make it happen. We do this in big ways, like with our relationships. We also do this in small ways, like when we crave sugar and search the pantry. On both ends of the spectrum we have a goal and do what it takes to accomplish it. If we want to be closer to our grandchildren, we don't ignore them and refuse to be involved in their lives. If we want to eat a sweet treat, we don't sit on the couch and wish it into existence.

The same is true about your relationship with God. If you want more of him, go get it. He is always available to you. God is not hiding from you. He is not evasive or difficult to find. He promises that if you are looking for him, you will not be disappointed. The key is that you must look. Put in the effort of knowing God, and you will find exactly what you are looking for.

Father, I want to be close to you. Help me to look for you with all my heart.

CORRECTION

Discipline your children, and they will give you peace;
they will bring you the delights you desire.

PROVERBS 29:17 NIV

Discipline can be a sticky topic for grandparents. We want to ensure that our grandchildren receive the benefits of godly parenting, but we don't always know how to do that when we aren't the primary caregivers. We've already raised our own kids and leading the next generation is completely new territory. Should we step in when we see a lack of discipline? Or is it best to not get involved?

Maybe as a parent you longed for extra help in raising and disciplining your own children. Maybe you endured situations where other people crossed a line and shared unwanted opinions. Regardless of your own experience, you can support your children in a way that works well for them. Humbly discuss your involvement with them and seek to honor what they ask for.

Father, thank you for equipping my children to raise their kids. Help me to support them well.

ALWAYS ATTENTIVE

LORD my God, I cried to you for help,
and you have healed me.

PSALM 30:2 ESV

God hears us whether we are praising him, requesting something, or crying out for his help. He hears us when our voices call out in anguish and when our spirit whispers his praise. His ears are always turned toward us, and we always have his full attention. He has not and will never miss a single detail of our lives. God's attentiveness is different from ours as parents or grandparents. The older children get, the less input we have in their lives. God's voice, on the other hand, is always relevant and necessary for all his children.

Whether you are 45 or 85, God hears your cries like a mother hears the cries of her infant. He is attentive to you and never leaves you. You don't mature past the point of needing his attention and his input. Approach him like a child, fully confident that what you say will be heard, acknowledged, and acted upon.

Father, help me to cry out to you for all my needs. I don't ever want to tire of asking you for help.

MOURNING TO JOY

We may weep through the night,
but at daybreak it will turn into shouts of ecstatic joy.

PSALM 30:5 TPT

There is no calamity on earth that lasts forever. Every awful, horrible thing that we experience is temporary. Just as the darkness of night gives way to the light of the morning, so our suffering will give way to the perfection of Christ. The only thing that lasts is the perfect and eternal love of God. This should bring us great joy! It should fill our hearts with hope and strengthen us to endure the difficulties we face in this life.

What does your nighttime weeping look like in this season? Whether you're dealing with an unexpected health crisis, a painful loss, or the anguish of watching your loved ones make poor choices, none of it will last forever. There will come a day when everything is perfect, good, and exactly how God intended it to be from the beginning. He will not leave you disappointed. He will turn your mourning into joy.

Father, help me to have an eternal perspective on the trials I am walking through.

FAITHFUL GOD

You have turned my mourning into joyful dancing.
You have taken away my clothes of mourning
and clothed me with joy.

Psalm 30:11 NLT

We experience awe and joy when we see the Lord working in our lives. Maybe that issue we prayed for has been resolved. Or the sin that held us prisoner has been forgiven, and God is helping us repair the damage. The tears that drenched our pillows have dried, and we awaken to a new morning. God is an expert at second chances and new beginnings. Nothing is impossible for him.

You will continue to face hardships in this life. Suffering may come but God can increase your faith and help you to develop perseverance. You serve an awesome God who provides a path through each challenge that comes your way. You can trust in him for guidance and deliverance. Whether in this world or the next, he will heal your wounds, clear away your sorrows, and soothe your pain.

Father, thank you for being so faithful to me.
Thank you for the eternal joy that you promise.

HUMBLE THANKSGIVING

How could I be silent when it's time to praise you?
Now my heart sings out, bursting with joy—
a bliss inside that keeps me singing,
"I can never thank you enough!"

Psalm 30:12 TPT

God is worthy of praise. Why would we ever withhold our thankfulness from him? Even if salvation was his only gift to us, he would still be worthy of all we have to give. He deserves shouts of joy and our eternal gratitude for the sacrifice of his perfect, sinless Son. He has showered his great mercy upon us and paid a debt that we could never have come close to reconciling.

No matter how long you've been following Jesus, your salvation will always be miraculous and undeserved. Christ's blood took you from death to life, from sin to salvation. You have gained everything you have only through the mercy and grace of God. Don't be haughty later in life, as though you have done the work yourself. Instead, continue to embrace your salvation with humility and thanksgiving.

I sing hallelujah to you, my father! Thank you for all you've done in my life.

DON'T COMPARE

Who can find a virtuous wife?
For her worth is far above rubies.

PROVERBS 31:10 NKJV

Many women feel intimidated by the woman in Proverbs 31. We read it as though it's a list of rules when instead, it's a pattern of principles. It was written as a poem, intended to inspire the king to make a wise choice in picking a wife. Instead, we tend to read it as a list of requirements that we can never measure up to. We can liken it to dreaming of a future spouse and imagining all the good things about them. Of course, they will embody some of those characteristics but it's unlikely that every single box will be checked.

It's not wrong to use Proverbs as inspiration but if it's become your highest standard for living then you've missed the mark. If you ask the Holy Spirit for guidance, he won't give you a list of things to work on. Instead, he will gently lead you toward truth and the repentance of sin as it is needed in your life. He will not overwhelm you with tasks to complete and boxes to check off.

Father, help me to be a woman who honors you. I want to follow your lead, not my own list of requirements.

REST WELL

The people of Israel shall keep the Sabbath, observing the Sabbath throughout their generations, as a covenant forever.

EXODUS 31: 16 ESV

After the first six days of creation, God honors his work by resting. He sets aside an entire day just for this purpose. It is an example for all of us to respect hard work and recognize the need to recharge. A day of rest allows us to reflect on what we have done in the previous days and prepare for what is to come. If we want to honor God with our work and our service, we need to learn how to rest well.

Rest can mean different things for different people, but the basic principles are the same. Take good care of your mind, body, and soul. This might mean taking a nap, turning off your phone, or taking a walk. Maybe for you it means listening to music you love or painting a picture. There isn't a clear definition of what it must be but the more we practice getting good rest, the healthier we will be.

Father, help me to rest well. I want to serve you with all my heart. Thank you for being concerned with the rest I need.

BLAMELESS ALREADY

God is a sun and shield;
the LORD bestows favor and honor;
no good thing does he withhold
from those whose walk is blameless.

PSALM 84:11 NIV

Every Christ follower has God's favor and protection. He promises to not withhold his goodness from his children. It might sound intimidating to read that he blesses those with a blameless walk. The reality is that if you are covered in the blood of Christ, you are already blameless. His righteousness is now yours. Furthermore, as you embrace this truth, your actions will surely follow.

In every stage of life, it's important to evaluate the state of your heart. Are you living as though work makes you good enough for God? Or are you leaning on the mercy of God, fully aware of your inability to measure up? God's favor is upon you not because of your goodness but because of the goodness of Christ.

Father, help me to embrace Christ's sacrifice and recognize that he is the only reason I can call myself blameless.

STRONG AND COURAGEOUS

Be strong, and let your heart be courageous,
all you who put your hope in the LORD.

PSALM 31:24 CSB

We've all comforted a child who is afraid. We say soothing words, stroke their hair, or hold them close. There is something in us as mothers and grandmothers that innately allows us to know how to provide comfort. Imagine how much more God can strengthen us when we need courage. He knows exactly what we need and is faithful to provide it. He wouldn't ask us to be strong and courageous if he couldn't back up what he's asking.

How many times have you felt the despair of a frustrating situation only to realize that you haven't asked God for help yet? It can be easy to forget that you have the creator of the universe on your side. There is nothing you will face that is too big, too complicated, or too hopeless for God. As you trust in him, he will strengthen you.

God, help me to be strong and courageous because of who you are.

HE GIVES

She opens her mouth with wisdom,
and the teaching of kindness is on her tongue.

PROVERBS 31:26 ESV

The Bible tells us that wisdom is more valuable than silver, gold, or rubies. Nothing we can ever desire compares with wisdom. So how do we acquire it? All we need to do is ask in faith. God promises that if we ask for wisdom, he will give it to us. There isn't a list of prerequisites or complicated steps to follow. Simply ask.

As a grandmother, you likely encounter many situations that require wisdom. You're trying to navigate the second half of your life, maintain relationships with adult children, keep your health in mind, deal with potential retirement and invest in your grandchildren. There is no way that any one person can handle all of this well on their own. You need God's wisdom. If you ask, he will surely give it to you. Ask him for help and he will help you navigate whatever you are facing.

Father, thank you for your generous and abundant wisdom! I trust that you will guide me as I follow you.

FEARING GOD

Charm is deceptive, and beauty does not last;
but a woman who fears the LORD will be greatly praised.

PROVERBS 31:30 NLT

We often use this verse to talk about the merits of inner beauty over outer beauty. We focus on the fact that the world sees our outwards appearance but God values what's in our hearts. We often glaze over the first part of the verse. *Charm is deceptive.* Charm doesn't necessarily have anything to do with the way that we look. The definition of charm is to captivate or arouse admiration. This is something we are warned against in the same sentence that we are warned about outward vanity.

Charm draws attention to yourself when you are called to draw attention to the Lord. Are you actively trying to win others to yourself or to God? Vanity is about more than the way you look. It stems from an attitude of your heart. Ask the Holy Spirit to reveal vanity in your life and respond with humility.

Father, I don't want to be full of vanity. Teach me how to revere who you are and put others above myself.

DON'T HIDE

I confessed all my sins to you
and stopped trying to hide my guilt.
I said to myself, "I will confess my rebellion to the LORD."
And you forgave me! All my guilt is gone.

PSALM 32:5 NLT

We've all seen a child sneak a cookie and then insist that they didn't do it. The crumbs on their face and the chocolate on their fingers gives them away. We think that this behavior is silly and chuckle at their obvious naughtiness. The truth is that we do the same thing all the time. We try to hide our sin from a god who is all knowing and all seeing. We are ashamed of ourselves even though God has never once shamed us.

When you make a mistake, run to God with the expectation that forgiveness is waiting for you. Stop trying to hide your sins and guilt. God is fully aware of your heart. He knows full well that you don't measure up to his standard of perfection. Your mistakes are not a surprise. He is waiting for you, full of mercy and grace.

Father, thank you for your forgiveness. I don't want to hide my sin from you.

ALWAYS THERE

You are my hiding place;
you protect me from trouble.
You surround me with songs of victory.

PSALM 32:7 NLT

God is constant in every season. No matter what changes in our lives, his position does not. He is always our safe place. He is always protecting us. He is always surrounding us with affection, security, and victory. When we get lost in a hectic season, get distracted by our own goals, or experience great trials, God never changes.

No matter what your life looks like right now, God is with you. He has never stopped protecting you from trouble. Ask him to open your eyes to the way that he has moved in your life. You will see that he is constant, steady, and unwavering even when you fail to notice.

Father, open my eyes to your presence in my life. Help me to see your faithfulness and protection.

GENTLE WITH FEAR

I prayed to the LORD, and he answered me.
He freed me from all my fears.

PSALM 34:4 NLT

The older that we get, the bigger our fears become. We worry about sickness, disaster, and loss. The fears of our grandchildren might seem silly in comparison but it's important to remember that the feeling is the same. Their fears reflect their reality, just like ours do. When we treat our grandchildren's fears with patience and kindness, we reflect the way that God handles our fears.

When your grandchildren are afraid it's easy to brush them off. Their fears are usually unrealistic, and you might not think that they matter. Instead of being flippant, remember that God is never cavalier with your fears. He is gentle, kind, and always listens. When your grandchildren are afraid you can do the same thing. You can be steady and kind as you teach them about the character of God.

Father, help me to be patient with my grandchildren. I want to teach them that you are patient and gentle with their fears.

TASTE AND SEE

Taste and see that the LORD is good;
blessed is the one who takes refuge in him.

PSALM 34:8 NIV

When it feels like the world is in a state of chaos, it can be easy to forget the goodness of God. No matter how discouraged we are by politics, world news, or cultural shifts, God is unchanging. When we focus only on the negative aspects of the world around us, we lose sight of God's constant goodness.

As you lead your family, let them see you revel in the goodness of God. It is good to pay attention to the reality of what is going on in the world, but it should not shake your faith or cause you to dwell on negativity. When you partake of God's goodness on a daily basis, you will notice that your perspective will shift, and you will experience more peace. As this happens, your family will see what it looks like to take refuge in the Lord despite the state of the world.

Father, I want to taste and see that you are good. No matter what happens around me, I want to take refuge in your presence.

GOD'S CHILD

Come, children of God, and listen to me.
I'll share the lesson I've learned of fearing the Lord.

PSALM 34:11 TPT

What a joy it is to be called a child of God. By faith in Christ, we are blessed to be adopted into God's heavenly kingdom. Our gratitude for being welcomed into God's family results in our consistent worship and praise. As we embrace our position as his beloved children, our lives will be transformed to reflect his character.

As a child of God, you have access to the creator of the universe. This is a great and wonderful privilege. You can be in his presence whenever you want. His presence is where you will find a true sense of belonging and satisfaction. Only through knowing your true identity as God's child will you be able to live abundantly.

God, thank you for being such a good father. Help me to embrace my position as your child and to seek your presence daily.

TAKE NOTICE

Your goodness is as high as the mountains.
Your justice is as deep as the great ocean.
LORD, you protect both people and animals.

PSALM 36:6 NCV

All of God's creation is good. From the rising sun to the way an oak tree stands, to the speckles in your grandchildren's eyes – it is all good. Every aspect of creation reflects God's character and teaches us about who he is. When we marvel at what he has made, we open our hearts to receive his goodness.

Today, look for aspects of creation that stir your heart in affection for your creator. Let yourself be moved by all that God has done and will continue to do. He has surrounded you with good things and he deserves all your praise. Slow down for a minute and take notice of the blessings in your life.

Father, help me to see your goodness. I don't want to be so busy that I miss what you are doing around me.

HE ALWAYS HELPS

Commit everything you do to the LORD.
Trust him, and he will help you.

PSALM 37:5 NLT

We've all experienced a grandchild insisting on doing a difficult task by themselves. As we watched them fumble, we wanted so badly to help. Sometimes, we jump in and show them the right way. Sometimes we know that it is best for them to learn how to conquer something on their own. We use different methods when we are helping our children to grow and mature. God does the same thing with us.

When you ask God for help, he may not always respond in exactly the way you want. Sometimes he will miraculously intervene and sometimes he will direct you step by step to accomplish something the way he knows is best. As his child, you can trust in his wisdom and remember that even if it doesn't look how you want, God is constantly helping you.

Father, help me to trust your wisdom and surrender my will. Thank you for always helping me when I ask.

HE IS DELIGHTED

When Yahweh delights in how you live your life,
he establishes your every step.

PSALM 37:23 TPT

Depending on our childhood experience, our view of what a good Father is might be skewed. Some of us had doting, kind fathers while some of us only know what it's like to experience harshness and impatience. God is a delightful Father. He is proud of his children. He watches us with joy and loves that we are his.

A proud father instills a sense of belonging and capability in his children. This is how God loves you. As you experience his love, you will see yourself with the right perspective. You'll see how strong, wonderful, and capable you are. If God is proud of you, you should be proud of yourself.

God, I want to see myself the way that you do. It's so sweet to know that you delight in me.

NEVER FORSAKEN

I was young and now I am old,
yet I have never seen the righteous forsaken
or their children begging bread.

Psalm 37:25 NIV

We are righteous because of what Christ has done on the cross. God will never turn his back on his Son and so he will never turn his back on those of us who belong to Jesus. It's impossible and would go against his nature. He promises to take care of his children, and he is incapable of breaking any of his promises.

Despite the hardship you may experience in this life, God has not forsaken you. You will be rewarded for your faithfulness, if not now, then in the days to come. You are promised an eternity of perfection and complete satisfaction. There is no trial that compares to the goodness that God has in store for you.

Jesus, thank you for never leaving my side. I know that you have not forsaken me.

NEVER ALONE

He stooped down to lift me out of danger
from the desolate pit I was in,
out of the muddy mess I had fallen into.
Now he's lifted me up into a firm, secure place
and steadied me while I walk along his ascending path.

PSALM 40:2 TPT

As a parent, and now as a grandparent, we've all helped children out of the various messes they get themselves into. We've bathed children covered head to toe in mud and we've bandaged scraped knees. We've turned the car around for forgotten homework and we've comforted the child who is struggling to manage their friendships. We could have told them to do it all on their own. We could have told them to handle their own messes. Instead, we willingly got involved even when it was inconvenient.

This is exactly how God loves you. He sees your messes and he dives right in. He doesn't leave you to your own devices or shame you for not being able to solve your own problems. He never insists that you fix things on your own.

Father, thank you for your constant help. Thank you that I am never alone and that you are always there to help.

DECLARE HIS GREATNESS

Many, LORD my God, are the wonders which you have done,
and your thoughts toward us;
there is none to compare with you.
If I would declare and speak of them,
they would be too numerous to count.

PSALM 40:5 NASB

Scripture makes it clear that God's mind is vastly different from ours. His ways are righteous and pure. His wisdom and strength are at a height we can never attain. His majesty is greater than we can comprehend. All these things should cause us to rejoice and stand in awe of him. As we practice reverence, it will spill out into every area of our lives.

If you ever feel stuck or lost in your relationship with God, reverence is a good place to return to. Think about how great God is and how nothing can compare to him. Let your heart worship him and dwell on the goodness of his character. As you focus your thoughts on him, you'll begin to grasp how much he loves you.

God, I know that your ways are higher than mine. Help me to live in reverence of you.

NO QUESTIONS

My God, I want to do what you want.
Your teachings are in my heart.

PSALM 40:8 NCV

Obedience is impossible without clear expectations. We've all seen this play out with the children in our lives. If they don't understand what we are asking, how can they possibly follow through? The same thing is true about our relationship with God. We cannot live a life that honors the Lord if we don't know what that means.

If you desire to do what God wants, you must have a clear understanding of what that is. The good news is that you are fully equipped with Scripture. Everything you need to know about living rightly is outlined in the Word. His teachings are fully available to you. You don't have to wonder what he wants or question how you are supposed to live.

Jesus, I want to be fully committed to your teachings. Help me to hide your Word in my heart.

GIVE FREELY

Oh, the joys of those who are kind to the poor!
The Lord rescues them when they are in trouble.
The Lord protects them
and keeps them alive.

Psalm 41:1-2 NLT

God always sides with the oppressed. He is gentle toward the marginalized and the forgotten. As such, he gives favor to those who behave in the same way. When we care for the poor, God promises to care for us. Sometimes, caring for others can seem inconvenient or burdensome. This shouldn't stop us from reflecting God's love to those who have less than we do. Knowing that God desires us to be kind and generous should motivate us to give freely of our time, resources, and energy.

As you care for the poor and the marginalized, your family will see you reap the joy that comes from service to God. Ask him to give you a soft heart and a willingness to display his love to everyone you meet. Take care of those who have less than you because you know that God will always take care of you.

God, I want to serve you well. Fill me with compassion and generosity. Help me teach my family how to be kind to the poor.

ON EAGLE'S WINGS

Those who trust in the LORD will find new strength.
They will soar high on wings like eagles.
They will run and not grow weary.
They will walk and not faint.

ISAIAH 40:31 NLT

On this earth, we are limited by our bodies. We grow older, we get tired, and we experience sickness. There is a day coming when we won't have any limitations. As we trust in God for our eternal salvation, we can look forward to perfection and unending goodness. With our limited perspective, we cannot comprehend all that God has in store for us.

No matter what the state of your health is, perfection is coming. You can look forward to that day with hope and great anticipation. As you live for the age to come, you can find security in the knowledge that God will renew your strength beyond anything you can image.

Jesus, thank you for the goodness you have in store for me. Help me to keep my eyes on you as I wait for Christ's return.

HE SUSTAINS

"Even to your old age and gray hairs
I am he, I am he who will sustain you.
I have made you and I will carry you;
I will sustain you and I will rescue you."

ISAIAH 46:4 NIV

For those of us in the second half of life, this verse reminds us of God's faithfulness. No matter the age we live to, God promises to be with us. He has carried us this far and he won't give up on us now. His nearness has never wavered, and it never will.

God has sustained you for all your days. From the moment that you came into this world, he has provided for you and watched over you. No matter how many gray hairs you have, God will never leave you. Your need for him is just as great as when you were a child. Lean on the strength that he provides and trust that he will continue to be faithful to you.

Father, thank you for your abundant care throughout every stage of my life.

SEPTEMBER

Teach us to number our days,
that we may present to You
a heart of wisdom.

Psalm 90:12 NASB

STEADY AND STILL

"Be still, and know that I am God.
I will be exalted among the nations,
I will be exalted in the earth!"

PSALM 46:10 ESV

God rarely shows up the way that we expect him to. When we think he'll be angry, he's gentle. When we think he'll be grandiose, he's quiet and lowly. When we think he'll be absent, he's consistent. His ways are not our ways. It goes against our instincts to find God in the stillness, yet he is there. When we calm our spirits and surrender our fight into the hands of God, surely, he will meet us there.

When your emotions feel like a tangled web and your spirit is unsettled, know that God is present. He is there, in the quiet, ready for you to lean on him. He will fight your battles if you let him. There is no need to let anxiety and confusion take over when the maker of the universe offers you peace. Instead, calm your heart, trust in his strength, and praise him for all that he does.

Thank you, Father, for fighting my battles, keeping me safe, and loving me extravagantly.

RESTORATION

Joseph said to his father, "They are my sons, whom God has given me in this place." And he said, "Please bring them to me, and I will bless them."

GENESIS 48:9 NKJV

Jacob grieved for his son Joseph for many years. He probably never imagined that his son wasn't actually dead. When they were reunited, Jacob had his joy renewed. Not only was he reunited with his son, but he was also able to meet his grandsons. What an incredible gift from God! Jacob's family had been broken but God brought restoration. He fixed an impossible situation.

Imagine how hopeless Jacob felt for all those years. His youngest son was gone, and his family was forever altered. If you are facing a difficult situation in your family, remember that your story isn't finished yet. God can take impossible situations and bring healing and restoration. When you feel hopeless, turn your eyes to the maker. Look to him for guidance and continue to trust that he is in control.

Father, thank you for your perfect plan for my life. Help me to trust you even when things seem impossible.

APPROACHABLE GOD

Purify me from my sins, and I will be clean;
wash me, and I will be whiter than snow.

PSALM 51:7 NLT

There are so many beautiful principles to be gleaned from the Psalms. We can learn to pray by reading the raw and emotional way the author approaches God. We see that we can go to him and ask directly for what we need. There is no mincing of words or complicated explanations needed. We don't need to say just the right thing or express ourselves perfectly.

Do you ever complicate your relationship with God? Instead, remember how remarkably simple it can be. Just go to him and tell him what you need. Spend time with him and let him lead you. As you embrace a life of simple commitment to your maker, your faith will be displayed for those around you. Your children and grandchildren will reap the rewards of your simple and honest approach to truth.

Father, thank you for being approachable. Help me to remember the simple glory of just being with you.

A LIGHT YOKE

"Take my yoke upon you and learn from me, for I am gentle and humble in heart, and you will find rest for your souls."

MATTHEW 11:29 NIV

Historically, a yoke was used to tether animals together for the purpose of work. When an animal is yoked, it is in servitude to its master. As we serve Jesus, we are yoked to him. His yoke is not burdensome like we might expect. Instead, he assures us that his yoke is light. When we do things his way, we will find freedom, not slavery.

God never intended for you to be weary and worn out. His intention for you is to have abundant life as you serve Jesus. If you feel like you cannot go on, it's time to ask him for wisdom. Maybe you've taken on more than necessary or are serving out of your own strength instead of God's. No matter what your task is, from being involved at church to caring for your grandchildren, God wants to refresh you and equip you well.

Jesus, thank you for giving me a light yoke. Help me to lean on you when I am overwhelmed.

TRUST IN HIM

When I am afraid,
I will put my trust in you.

PSALM 56:3 NLT

When something frightens our grandchildren, we move quickly toward them. Their anguished cries are the last thing we want to hear. We don't want them to be afraid or in pain. We long for them to know that Grandma is always there and will protect them from harm. In the same way, God is near to us when we are afraid. We can be assured of his ability to keep us safe.

What are your greatest fears right now? They probably look different from when you were a little girl, a teenager, or even a young woman. Each season of life brings new challenges and waters you've never navigated before. No matter how unfamiliar your terrain is, there is one thing that never changes. You can always put your trust in God. He does not scoff at your fear or tell you to get over it. Instead, he embraces you and equips you. He comforts you and gives you your daily bread.

Father, help me have unwavering faith in your care. I want to trust you with my fears.

FULLY KNOWN

"Before I formed you in the womb I knew you,
before you were born I set you apart."

JEREMIAH 1:5 NIV

Just as our children were known by God before they were ever in the womb, so has god known our grandchildren. He chose them as his children and set them apart. He knew exactly who they would be and what each day of their life would look like. There is nothing about them that surprises him or throws him off.

What a gift for your grandchildren to grow up with a strong sense of belonging. You can remind them of who they truly are, speaking truth over them and affirming their identity in Christ. Remind them that they are fully known and fully loved by their creator.

God, I love that you knew us before we came to exist. Help my grandchildren know how deeply they are loved.

YOUR STRONG TOWER

Trust in him at all times, you people;
pour out your hearts to him,
for God is our refuge.

Psalm 62:8 NIV

We love it when our grandchildren run to us and jump in our laps. The cuddling and the giggling are precious memories. We want to be seen as steady and safe. If our grandchildren feel protected and loved in our presence, we know that we have done a good job. God views us in the same way. He wants us to know that he is trustworthy. He wants us to know that we are safe in his presence.

Just as you desire for your grandchildren to experience security in your presence, so does God want you to feel safe with him. He is your strong tower, your refuge, and your protector. You can run to him with abandon and expectation, just like your grandchildren run to you.

Father, thank you for your constant presence in my life. Help me to trust you for strength and security.

UNENDING NEED

"People do not live by bread alone, but by every word that comes from the mouth of God."

MATTHEW 4:4 NLT

The longer we experience something, the easier it is to take it for granted. Over the span of a marriage, we might stop noticing the little gestures that add up to a lifetime of love. Over the length of a friendship, we might take for granted how lovely it is to have someone regularly checking in on us. In our relationship with God, we can easily forget how vital it is to hear God's Word.

At this point in your relationship with God, are you still valuing his Word? It's important to view it as necessary as you did when you were first walking with him. His Word is what sustains you, encourages you, and protects you. You cannot live fully without it. Today, ask God to give you fresh affection for his Word.

Father, thank you for your life-giving Word! I want to lean on your strength every day.

AWESOME IN DEED

Come and see the works of God;
He is awesome in His doing toward
The sons of men.

PSALM 66:5 NKJV

When the Israelites were enslaved in Egypt, God rescued them in mighty ways. Nothing could stand in the way of his plans. There was no ruler too great, no sea too impassable, no human too flawed to ruin what God had set into motion. His faithfulness to the Israelites, even when they were stubborn and turned away from him, should encourage us. It should compel us to trust his work in our own lives.

No matter what obstacles you see in your life, God can overcome them. He is not limited by your perspectives, your flaws, or your lack of faith. As you trust in him, he will strengthen you and encourage you. His ways are greater than yours and everything he does is trustworthy. He has been, and will be, awesome in his deeds toward you and each generation to come.

Father, thank you for your greatness. Thank you for all of the wonderful things you've done in my life.

STAND CONFIDENTLY

Each one must answer for himself and give a personal account of his own life before God.

ROMANS 14:12 TPT

As mothers, and now grandmothers, our lives are intricately linked to our family. As children grow, it can be difficult to let them go. We spend so much time keeping them close, that the inevitable separation can feel abrupt and painful. We must remember that our greatest goal is not for them to be close to us, but for them to be close to God.

At the end of the day, your children and grandchildren are accountable for themselves. You have the privilege of interceding for them and equipping them as best you can. You can encourage them in their relationship with God and teach them how to honor him. As the matriarch of your family, your greatest goal should be for your family to stand confidently before the Lord.

Father, I want my family to know and honor you. Help me to point them toward you in all that I do.

AGE WELL

Don't discard me in my old age.
As my strength fails, do not abandon me.

PSALM 71:9 CSB

We live in a society that does not always value the aging process. There is unending pressure to stay young, both in the way that we look and in how we contribute to the world. The world tells us to look younger, never stop working, and make sure we do it all with grace. This message does not align with Scripture. God places great value on getting older. He says that glory is found in our later years.

Whether you are a young grandparent, or are well past midlife, surely you have felt the pressure found with getting older. In these years, ask God for his perspective on your life. Don't let society pressure you into feeling that you have lost worth or value. The opposite is true, the faithfulness that you have displayed throughout your life is precious to God.

Father, thank you for your love that continues all of my days. I want to be confident in how you've made me, no matter my age.

WE SHALL SEE JESUS

Better a day in your courts
than a thousand anywhere else.
I would rather stand at the threshold of the house of my God
than live in the tents of wicked people.

PSALM 84:10 CSB

Oh, what glory will surround us once we get to our eternal home. Delight will be constant as we gaze on the face of our wonderful Savior. Freedom from pain, illness, sin, and the enemy will cause us to worship God's holy name for eternity. We'll be exactly who he designed us to be, and we'll see everything with the same perfect perspective that he does.

No matter what your life has looked like, you can look forward to eternity with great anticipation. If you've walked through great suffering, complete comfort and perfection are coming. Even if your life has been relatively free of trials, know that your best day still cannot be compared to the goodness that is to come.

Jesus, I long for you to return. I want to spend all my days in your glorious presence.

DO NOT FRET

Rest in the LORD, and wait patiently for Him;
Do not fret because of him who prospers in his way.

PSALM 37:7 NKJV

We often want to see God move in our own timing. We assume that we understand enough about our situation that we should be able to decide what is best. The truth is that our understanding is nowhere near as sophisticated as God's. Instead of worrying about how something will work out, we should rest and wait patiently.

If you are waiting on the Lord for something, especially something big, keep on trusting! Don't give up. Even when it looks hopeless, or you see others succeeding before you, stay steady. God's timing is perfect, even when we don't understand it. Lean on him and ask him to give you the grace to wait.

Thank you, Lord, for being a good Father who always moves on our behalf. I know that I can rely on you and trust in your timing.

GROW IN GENEROSITY

"Truly, I tell you, this poor widow has put in more than all of them. For they all contributed out of their abundance, but she out of her poverty put in all she had to live on."

LUKE 21:3-4 ESV

God doesn't need our money to see his plans succeed. We don't give because God depends on us; we give because God knows that a generous heart is thankful and soft. When we are generous with what have, we acknowledge that it isn't truly ours. We put ourselves in a position to depend more fully on God and we humbly admit that the needs of others are just as important as our own.

Today, ask God how you can grow in generosity. In this season of your life, you may be tempted to waver in the way that you give. Remember that we are asked to be open handed with our blessings in every season of life.

Father, help me give my best with a pure motive like the widow in Scripture. Give me opportunities to be generous with what you've given me.

SHARE GOODNESS

I will sing of the graciousness of the LORD forever;
to all generations I will make your faithfulness known
with my mouth.

PSALM 89:1 NASB

God is gracious toward his children. He leads us like sheep to green pastures. He provides for us faithfully and he protects us when we are weak. All good things come from his hands. It is good and right to talk about the goodness of God. When we normalize talking about what he's done, we normalize a relationship with him that is focused on consistent, daily interactions.

Tell your family about God's goodness. Talk about what he has done and how he has been faithful to you. Don't keep those stories to yourself. Let them seep into the conversations you have as naturally as you might talk about the weather or what you've been reading lately. As you share in a non-complicated way, your family will see that a relationship with God is simple and lovely.

God, may my mouth sing your praises all my days. Help me to share your goodness and faithfulness with my family.

PRIVILEGED TO SUFFER

Instead, be very glad—for these trials make you partners with Christ in his suffering, so that you will have the wonderful joy of seeing his glory when it is revealed to all the world.

1 PETER 4:13 NLT

When we suffer, we build a strong character, and we become more like Christ. While suffering is painful, it is also beneficial. When this is our perspective, we will still suffer but we won't despair. We are filled with hope knowing that God's plans are better than ours and that we can weather any storm.

The goodness of suffering is a difficult concept for young believers. As someone with more experience you can encourage your grandchildren to embrace the benefit of suffering. If you think about it, you can probably recall several trials that impacted you positively in the long run. Suffering is never enjoyable while it's happening but the fruit that it can eventually bring is valuable.

Jesus, thank you for the privilege of sharing in your suffering. Help me to encourage my grandchildren when they go through trials.

SHELTER AND STRENGTH

Those who live in the shelter of the Most High will find rest in the shadow of the Almighty.

PSALM 91:1 NLT

Why do we waste time worrying about things that will probably never happen? We relive stressful scenarios in our minds and envision situations that may never come to pass. We engage in fretting even when God consistently offers us his protection and peace. Instead of drowning in our own anxiety, we can rest in the shadow of the Almighty.

As you learn to surrender your fears to the Lord, you can lead your family in the same way. Your grandchildren will face just as many, if not more, difficulties in their lives and you have the privilege of helping to equip them. You can show them what it looks like to rely on the Lord even when the storms of life are pummeling you.

Father, teach me to run to you, knowing that only you can help me.

GIVE WISELY

"Where your treasure is,
there your heart will be also."

MATTHEW 6:21 NIV

We know that how we spend our money says a lot about us. It reveals what we think is most valuable and what our habits are. We are wise when we teach our children and grandchildren how to manage their finances well. It can be tempting to shower our grandchildren with gifts, but this might not always be the best route to take.

If you don't want to teach your grandchildren that material items are to be continuously sought after, then maybe abundant gift giving isn't ideal. Ask God for wisdom in how to handle this area of being a grandparent. Honor the wishes of your adult children and consider that presents are not the only way to show your love.

Father, help me make wise financial decisions. Show me how I can support my children and grandchildren in this area.

ALWAYS VALUABLE

They will still bear fruit in old age,
healthy and green.

PSALM 92:14 CSB

Though we may see ourselves as less productive, God says that we will still bear fruit in our old age. We have immense value no matter how negatively the world views the aging process. Our worth in God's eyes has not changed. His opinion of us has never been tied to what we can accomplish, and it stays steady even when we feel less useful.

If you find yourself in the later years of your life, wondering how you're supposed to gauge success, rest in the fact that your very existence is a delight to the Lord. He doesn't want your worth to be defined by how much you can get done and what you can do for others. Instead, your very being is of great value to the Lord. Your service, accomplishments, and the accolades of others don't mean anything compared to his great love for you.

Father, help me serve you with greater passion in my later years. Help me to have your perspective on getting older.

TWO MASTERS

"No one can serve two masters. Either you will hate the one and love the other, or you will be devoted to the one and despise the other. You cannot serve both God and money."

MATTHEW 6:24 NIV

Can you imagine having two full-time jobs and trying to devote equal effort and energy to both? One or both will surely suffer. It's impossible to do both with the same level of excellence, if at all. This scripture describes trying to love both God and money. One of them will always come out on top. You cannot idolize money while keeping God on his rightful throne in your life.

Even as a grandparent, with many years of life experience behind you, it is never too late to make positive changes. If you have spent your time idolizing money over the Lord, repent and ask for forgiveness. There is never a point in your life when you cannot change your habits or the way that you think. You always have what you need to further align your thinking with Scripture.

Father, thank you for the finances you have blessed me with. I want to honor you with the way that I view money.

PRAY SCRIPTURE

Let us come to him with thanksgiving.
Let us sing psalms of praise to him.

PSALM 95:2 NLT

We all have days when prayer feels tiring or laborious. Our minds can be weary, and our thoughts can feel jumbled or messy. When this happens, it's important to remember that we can communicate with God even if we don't know what to say. We can read Scripture and pray for what we find within the pages. It is good to agree with the words of others and thank God for all that he's done.

It's easy to forget that your prayers don't have to be perfect. You don't have to communicate with God in the same way that you communicate with the people. You don't have to wonder if what you say will be perceived properly or if you're going to be understood. You don't have to worry about offending him or saying something incorrectly. Instead, rely on Scripture and let your heart commune freely with his.

Father, thank you for the reminder that prayer can be simple. Help me to communicate freely with you.

SIMPLE GOSPEL

He forgives all my sins
and heals all my diseases.

PSALM 103:3 NCV

We have done nothing to deserve the goodness that God lavishes on us. We are free from condemnation because of what Christ has done on the cross. His blood has made us clean, and we no longer have to fear death. There is nothing so horrible that it cannot be forgiven and there is no sickness so great that God cannot heal it. This is the glorious mystery of the gospel.

As you seek to disciple your family, remember that this truth is at the core of everything you believe. It's easy to get lost in the dos and don'ts of Christianity but nothing comes close to being as important as a deep understanding of Christ's sacrifice and forgiveness. When you are tempted to focus on behavior, remember that the core of gospel matters more.

Jesus, I don't ever want to get over the basics of the gospel. Help me to prioritize Jesus' sacrifice over the behavior of others.

TRUE BELONGING

We have been made right in God's sight by faith, we have peace with God because of what Jesus Christ our Lord has done for us.

ROMANS 5:1 NLT

The moment we put our trust in Jesus, we are made right before God. Christ's perfection becomes our perfection, and we get to claim his righteousness as our own. We are no longer bound by our weaknesses and limited by our lack of ability. We can confidently and unashamedly approach God because our sin is no longer in the way. Christ's sacrifice grants us eternal belonging.

Today's generation of young people is searching desperately for belonging. They are so hungry for validation and a sense of security. As a believer, you know exactly where true belonging is found. When the opportunity arises, you can share this great hope with the young people in your life. Remind them that no matter what the world says, God is the source of all that they are searching for.

God, thank you for the security that I have in Jesus. Help me to share your love with my grandchildren.

FAITHFUL LOVE

The LORD is compassionate and gracious,
slow to anger and abounding in faithful love.

PSALM 103:8 CSB

God's love is faithful. This means that it is unchanging despite circumstances. Faithfulness cannot have conditions. If God's love is faithful then that means that it is unwavering, unchanging and does not depend on our abilities. When we understand God's faithfulness, we cannot help but respond with authenticity and thanksgiving.

If you've lived most of your life believing that God's love was dependent on your actions, it's time to rest in his faithfulness. Take a deep breath and realize that you are enough simply because you are his child. His love for you does not change when you fail or when you succeed. If there's a little part of your heart that is still convinced that you need to perform to earn God's love, ask him to give you fresh understanding of his faithfulness.

Father, thank you for your faithfulness. Give me a fresh revelation of your love for me.

DON'T JUDGE

"Do not judge,
or you too will be judged."

MATTHEW 7:1 NIV

Sometimes, the older we get, the more judgmental we become. Having lived through a myriad of experiences, we really should become more merciful and accepting. Instead, it's really easy to become set in our ways. We assume that we know best, and that other people should live according to our own rules. This way of thinking does not align with Scripture.

If your thoughts are filled with a lot of *they should* phrases, maybe it's time to reconsider the value you place on your own opinion. The good news is that even if you've spent your entire life wrongfully judging others, Christ is still merciful. He is delighted by your desire to soften your heart. He will faithfully lead you with gentleness and kindness toward the right way of thinking.

Father, forgive me judging those around me. Soften my heart and help me to see others with mercy and kindness.

DON'T FORGET

They soon forgot what he had done
and did not wait for his plan to unfold.

Psalm 106:13 NIV

It is wise to remember what God has done in our lives. Sometimes we move so quickly to our next desire that we don't even take the time to thank him for providing for us. Our memories of his kindness should not get pushed to the back of our minds. We should be intentional to praise God for all that he has done.

Think about all the things that God has accomplished in your life. Make a list of the ways that he has been faithful to you. Thank him for his goodness and the blessings that he has so abundantly given you. Remember that there are probably parts of your present life that are answers to past prayers.

Father, I want to pay attention to how you move in my life. Help me to notice all that you do and to have a posture of thanksgiving.

HURTFUL FRIENDS

They reward me evil for good,
and hatred for my love.

PSALM 109:5 ESV

We don't usually expect to be hurt by someone we consider a friend. Yet, bad choices are sometimes made, and betrayal is a crushing blow to our spirits. It is difficult to recover from the hurt that comes from someone we trust. Despite how much it hurts, we are called to respond with humility and grace.

If you've ever been hurt by a friend, you know how painful it is. Your heart probably felt raw and vulnerable. In those situations, it's best to be humbly led by the Holy Spirit. He will keep you soft and open to the direction of the Lord. As you embrace humility, you'll be able to more readily forgive the wrongs of others. This isn't always easy, but it is the way of Christ. He understands being the target of ill treatment more than anyone else ever can.

Father, help me to be gracious when the actions of others are hurtful. I never want to repay evil for evil.

FAITHFUL OBEDIENCE

It was by faith that Noah built a large boat to save his family from the flood. He obeyed God, who warned him about things that had never happened before.

HEBREWS 11:7 NLT

As passersby watched Noah build the ark, they assumed he was crazy. Up until then the earth had been watered from the ground up. No one had ever seen a single drop of rain. Noah had to listen to the accusations of his neighbors and still faithfully follow God's instructions. He stayed faithful and was obedient to God's directions even when it didn't make sense.

There will be times in your life when the opinions of others tempt you to stray from God's path. It's difficult to do something when everyone around you disagrees. Even then, trust that God will not lead you astray. He knows what is best for you and has been faithful to lead you up until now.

Father, give me faith like Noah. Help me to be obedient even when it doesn't make sense to other people.

CHERISH WISDOM

The fear of the LORD is the beginning of wisdom;
all who follow his instructions have good insight.
His praise endures forever.

PSALM 111:10 CSB

When we fear the Lord, we respect him and recognize that he is far greater than we are. We humbly admit that we need his love, support, and direction in every aspect of our lives. We ask for wisdom because we know that without his guidance, we are lost.

The presence of Godly wisdom has a ripple effect on our families. When we honor the Lord with our lives, our children will benefit, and their children will benefit. When we treat wisdom as the treasure that it is, we teach our families to do the same. They will see the benefit that comes from wisdom and will seek it out on their own.

Father, thank you for the gift of wisdom. Give my children and grandchildren a hunger for wisdom and a desire to follow your instructions.

EMOTIONAL MATURITY

They won't be afraid of bad news;
their hearts are steady because they trust the LORD.

PSALM 112:7 NCV

No one likes receiving bad news. Whether it's a minor disappointment or a tragic situation, we would prefer to shy away from trouble. When we rely on ourselves for the right response to trouble, we set ourselves up for failure. Instead, we should rely on God's strength. He can give us the ability to find peace amid difficulties.

Steady, healthy emotions are a mark of maturity and trust in the Lord. It's common for young people to flounder a bit in this area. Often, as they navigate life's struggles for the first time, they may feel lost in a storm of emotions. When you display peace in the presence of bad news, you show them what it looks like to rely on the Lord's steadiness. Remind them that maturity takes time.

Father, I know that you are the one who keeps me steady in the presence of bad news. Help me to teach my grandchildren how to rely on you.

OCTOBER
Continue in the things you have learned and become convinced of, knowing from whom you have learned them.
2 Timothy 3:14 NASB

MAKE PEACE

"Blessed are the peacemakers,
for they shall be called the sons of God."

MATTHEW 5:9 ESV

As parents we had plenty of opportunities to be peacemakers. The same is true about being a grandparent. The biggest difference is that as grandparents, we aren't faced with the everyday pressures of being the main caregiver. We can help our grandchildren manage conflict in a way that might have been much more taxing when we were the parents.

As a grandparent, you can likely approach conflict differently than you did with your own kids. You're probably more removed from the situation and have the benefit of being well rested. Take this opportunity to be levelheaded, patient, and full of grace. Remember what it was like to deal with constant squabbles and seek to be lifegiving for your adult children.

Jesus, help me to be a peacemaker in my own family. I want to bless my family and help them handle conflict well.

HE BRINGS VICTORY

Not to us but to your name be the glory,
because of your love and faithfulness.

PSALM 115:1 NIV

God makes the impossible possible. Even though he is fully capable of accomplishing his will, he invites us to work alongside him. When he brings victory, we must guard against becoming puffed up. We must stay aware of our weakness compared to his great strength. It isn't right to take credit for the work of the Lord in our lives.

You may be tempted to take credit for the good things in your life. Remember that it is always God's hand in your life that makes things possible. He is the one who puts breath in your lungs, and he is the one who gives you the ability to succeed in the first place. When your relationships thrive, thank God. When you reach goals at work, thank God. No matter what success looks like in your life, God is worthy of the credit. Ask him to keep your heart soft and free of pride.

Thank you, Father, for including me in your kingdom work. I praise you and you alone for the goodness in my life.

TRUST THE PROCESS

You have been believers so long now that you ought to be teaching others. Instead, you need someone to teach you again the basic things about God's word. You are like babies who need milk and cannot eat solid food.

Hebrews 5:12 NLT

Sometimes, without realizing it, we expect others to know something that took us months or even years to learn. God has each of us on a different path. It is hasty and even prideful to assume that everyone around us should learn the same things at the same time as us.

You can apply this principle to your relationships with your children and grandchildren. Remember that in the early days of your faith, you likely believed differently than you do now. Your faith has grown and matured into what it is today. You didn't learn everything at once and you didn't learn without making mistakes. Let your family grow at the pace that God has for them.

Father, I don't want to rush my loved ones in their spiritual growth. Help me to be patient and trust that you are always at work.

EXPRESS GRATITUDE

Give thanks to the LORD, for he is good;
his love endures forever.

PSALM 118:1 NIV

It is good to take time to thank God for all that he has done in our lives. From waking us up in the morning, to providing for our families, to keeping the earth rotating perfectly, his goodness is everywhere. When we actively take note of what he has done for us, we posture our hearts to be continuously aware of his faithfulness.

Do you ever fall into the trap of compartmentalizing the work of God? Just because you haven't received an answer for a specific prayer, does not mean that God is not steadily at work in your life. Today, take some time to thank him for all that he's done. If you pay attention, you will start to see his goodness all around you.

Father, I know that you are constantly at work.
Help me to see your faithfulness in my life.

ALWAYS GROWING

Do not rebuke mockers or they will hate you;
rebuke the wise and they will love you.

PROVERBS 9:8 NIV

In a society that elevates arguments and opinions, it's easy to fall into the pattern of constantly having something to say. Especially as we get older, we tend to become set in our ways and are less likely to change the way we think. While maturity is good, lack of growth is not. We are not meant to be stagnant thinkers. Instead, we should approach the world around us with humility, always ready to admit that we might be wrong.

The wise love rebuke because they are always willing to grow and change. When you aspire to be wise, you will also love correction. There is not an age limit for walking with humility and growing in wisdom. Even as a grandparent, at this stage of your life, you can have a soft heart that is willing to change when you are wrong.

Father, I won't ever want to be rigid and unchanging. Soften my heart and teach me how to love growth and wisdom.

WELL EQUIPPED

How can a young person live a pure life?
By obeying your word.

Psalm 119:9 NCV

As culture changes, we may feel despair when we think about the world that our grandchildren are growing up in. We might wonder how they are supposed to combat the temptation we see everywhere or how they are supposed to remain strong in a world that is full of evil. The truth is that because of God's Word, they are well equipped to handle any trial or temptation. Even when the World comes crashing down, his Word will remain steady forever.

Though culture shifts, God's Word remains. You can help your grandchildren navigate things you have not experienced because you both have access to the unchanging Word of God. You can teach them how to seek wisdom and how to apply scripture to their lives. No matter what they are facing, God's Word is strong enough to help them succeed.

Father, give my grandchildren a desire to read your Word. Equip them to navigate the world they live in.

ADMIT WRONGS

Confess your sins to each other and pray for each other so that you may be healed. The prayer of a righteous person is powerful and effective.

JAMES 5:16 NIV

Confessing our sins to each other is a habit that must be developed. If we don't do this consistently then it can feel forced or even awkward. Instead, we can choose to create an atmosphere in our homes where it is normal to consistently admit our wrongs, ask for forgiveness, and move forward in a healthy way.

If this wasn't something you did with your own children, it is never too late to start. When you consistently admit that you are wrong, you give others the freedom to do the same. You can display your need for mercy daily by refusing to hide your sins in shame. As you embrace your lack of perfection, you create an atmosphere of freedom that your children and grandchildren will benefit from.

God, give me enough humility to admit when I am wrong. Help my family to walk in freedom as we embrace your mercy.

TURN TO HIM

My life's strength melts away with grief and sadness;
come strengthen me and encourage me with your words.

PSALM 119:28 TPT

We've all been through seasons of great pain and grief. No matter the details, suffering is the great equalizer. At some point or another, despite status or success, we are all laid bare by pain. As followers of Jesus, we are assured that he will comfort us in this life and will wipe away our sorrows in the next.

The way that you cope with grief and sadness is what sets you apart. The presence of trials is inevitable and has no correlation to your faith. What matters is how you deal with it. Do you call upon the Lord in your distress? Or do you seek out comfort on your own? No matter what you are facing, God wants to encourage you with his Word and equip you to walk steadily through your trial.

God, I want to rely on you when trouble comes. When I am full of sadness or grief, remind me to turn to you for encouragement.

STRONG AND COURAGEOUS

"Be strong and very courageous. Be careful to obey all the instructions Moses gave you. Do not deviate from them, turning either to the right or to the left. Then you will be successful in everything you do."

JOSHUA 1:7 NLT

The Word is full of instructions to be strong and courageous. God does not give this command lightly or without foundation. He does not tell us to be strong because he thinks that we can do things on our own. Instead, he commands us to be strong and courageous because he himself has already equipped us with what we need. He has given us every tool and instruction necessary for success.

As a grandmother, you can display God's strength for your grandchildren. Instead of showing them your success, show them how God has equipped you to be brave and conquer each trial you have faced. Teach them that strength and courage don't have to be mustered up when they come from a place of reliance on God's ability.

God, thank you for giving me strength. Thank you that I can be courageous because you are on my side.

EACH GENERATION

The LORD is good;
His mercy is everlasting,
And His truth endures to all generations.

PSALM 100:5 NKJV

As we navigate the grandparenting season of life, we may begin to forget that we were once a grandchild. We were once the youngest, most vulnerable member of the family and our own grandparents may have wondered if they were doing a good enough job in their roles. God has been faithful to each generation of our family.

It is good to remember that we are not central in the story of the world. God's faithfulness began long before we were here, and it will continue for all of eternity. Your worries, though new to you, are not new to God. He carried your ancestors through each day of their lives, he has carried you, and he will faithfully carry each of your grandchildren. Find peace in knowing that you are part of a story much larger than just yourself.

Father, give me your perspective. When I am overwhelmed, remind me of your faithfulness throughout the ages.

TEARS TO JOY

Those who plant in tears
will harvest with shouts of joy.

Psalm 126:5 NLT

God is very aware of our tears. He knows our deepest hurts and he hears us when we cry out to him. Our tears are not overlooked or ignored. In fact, God promises that he will turn our tears into joy. We are assured that nothing is wasted in the kingdom of heaven. God will faithfully honor and heal our worst heartaches.

Trust that God sees you and notices when you are hurting. When your grandchildren need comfort, you can share with them that the God of the entire universe sees each tear that falls from their eyes. He sees them clearly and knows them well. Share with them the times that he has turned your tears into joy and then watch as he is faithful to them in the same way.

Father, thank you for holding my tears so tenderly. Thank you for taking my sadness and giving me joy.

EVERY CIRCUMSTANCE

I have learned to be content
in whatever circumstances I am.

PHILIPPIANS 4:11 NASB

We admire Paul's contentment because we know that his circumstances were often dire and seemingly hopeless. Even though he had every reason to despair, he trusted in the Lord and continued on the path set before him. We aren't facing intense persecution, death, or imprisonment. If Paul could remain hopeful, then surely, we can too.

Maybe being a grandmother is harder than you thought it would be. Maybe this season of your life doesn't look the way you hoped. No matter what trial you face, you can be content in this season. You can lean on the Lord's strength and trust in him for provision. Today, surrender your expectations and perceptions to God. Ask him how you can honor him exactly where you're at, even if circumstances don't change.

God, help me to be content in every circumstance. I want to honor you no matter what is going on in my life.

YOUR GREAT GIFT

Children are God's love-gift;
they are heaven's generous reward.

Psalm 127:3 TPT

Children are a gift from the Lord. They are a blessing and a treasure. This doesn't change simply because they become parents themselves. When our children become parents, it can seem tempting to turn all our attention to the presence of babies. While babies are worthy of our greatest affections, remember that our children are still a great and beautiful gift.

When you add the role of grandmother to the description of your life, you don't trade in the role of mother. You are just as needed as ever. While your relationship with your adult children changes, don't forget that they are still God's gift to you, no matter their age or season of life. Cherish them, encourage them, and esteem them as God's beloved treasure. You are still their greatest cheerleader, their wise helper, and their caring advocate. You can respect their adulthood while still being a gracious mother.

Father, teach me how to love my adult children well. Show me how to encourage them and support them in this season of their lives.

HIS AFFECTION

Give thanks to the LORD, for he is good,
for his steadfast love endures forever.

PSALM 136:1 ESV

Trying to understand the goodness of God is like trying to fully comprehend the nature of eternity. Our minds simply can't grasp that he is good through and through, all the time. God's love is so much greater than we can ever fathom. When we are stumped or baffled by God's goodness, it should lead us to thanksgiving.

Thank the Lord for who he is. Thank him for what he's done in your life and all that he will do. Thank him for showing up when you didn't realize it and thank him for protecting you all your days. Let his praises flow from your lips and watch as your life becomes a testimony to his goodness. When you are thankful in all circumstances, your family will reap the benefits.

Father, fill my heart with praises for you. Help me to always be aware of your steadfast love.

WORKING FOR HIM

A hard worker has plenty of food,
but a person who chases fantasies has no sense.

Proverbs 12:11 NLT

The Word is clear in its instruction to work hard. There is wisdom in working hard at whatever God has placed in our path. This applies to our relationships, our jobs, and the way that we manage our resources. We can have the best intentions in the world but if we don't work toward our goals, our intentions are meaningless. We can intend to be an excellent mother or grandmother, but if we don't diligently work at it, we display foolishness.

There is great reward in working hard and accomplishing a goal. It takes hard work to maintain healthy relationships and they don't happen by accident. You must cultivate humility, be diligent in prayer, and seek to honor the Lord in the way you communicate. As you work on these things, you can be assured that God will provide the rest.

Father, please instill your work ethic in me. I want to be diligent in tending to my relationships.

KEEP YOUR WORD

You keep every promise you've ever made to me!
Since your love for me is constant and endless,
I ask you, Lord, to finish every good thing
that you've begun in me!

PSALM 138:8 TPT

God is true to his Word. He always keeps his promises. It is wise to do our best to reflect this aspect of his character. Children watch adults to see if they keep their word. We, as grandmas and believers, have a special place in the lives of our grandchildren. Our words matter. We should do our best to keep our promises and be reliable.

When you are true to your word, you reflect the character of God. As the original promise keeper, he can equip you to be successful in this area as well. No matter what your tendency has been in the past, God can help you to be a woman who is true to her word. Ask him for wisdom and he will give it to you in abundance.

Father, help me to be a woman of my word. I want my family to be able to depend on what I say.

KNOWN AND LOVED

LORD, you have examined my heart
and know everything about me.

PSALM 139:1 NLT

God knows everything about us. There is nothing about us that surprises him or causes him confusion. We are each fully known, and yet fully loved. His love for us is all knowing and all encompassing. In our humanity, our love is often conditional and has limits. We aren't always capable of loving others when we discover the darkest parts of who they are. God's love on the other hand, has no limits.

As a grandmother, you get to display the limitless love of God for your grandchildren. This may feel effortless when a sweet little baby is sitting on your lap. Later, this may feel challenging as children grow and potentially make decisions you disagree with. In both situations, ask God for wisdom and that he would teach you to love like he does.

Father, thank you for loving me even though you see me at my worst. Help me to love others in the same way.

CHERISH CHILDREN

"Let the little children come to me, and do not hinder them, for the kingdom of God belongs to such as these."

MARK 10:14 NIV

Children are a great blessing. Scripture is clear that they are to be protected and cherished. They are not a burden or an annoyance, but instead should be elevated above us. Jesus welcomed children openly even when the disciples assumed he had more important work to do. In Christ's eyes, the children were the most important work. The way that we view them reveals the state of our heart.

Have you noticed that the children in your life tend to reveal your weaknesses? Maybe you struggled as a parent and you're unsure how you'll manage being a grandparent. It takes humility, patience, and selflessness to care for children well. If these things aren't present in your heart, being a caregiver will reveal it. Ask God to strengthen you and give you his perspective. His love for children is so great, he will not hesitate to equip you to love them well.

Father, help me to love the children in my life. I know how precious they are, and I want to love them like you do.

ALWAYS SEEN

Your eyes saw me when I was formless;
all my days were written in your book and planned
before a single one of them began.

PSALM 139:16 CSB

Each of our days is seen by God. He knows every detail of our lives. When we sat on our grandparents' laps, he knew what our own grandchildren would look like. He has woven together a generational story that is more complex than we can imagine. He sees all of time instantaneously yet is fully aware of each of his beloved children.

Your days are known, planned, and ordered. God planned the existence of each of your grandchildren before you ever thought about them. Each one of them is the intentional, wonderful, and purposeful work of God. Even on difficult days, when you aren't sure how to navigate your relationships, you can find security in knowing that you are their grandmother on purpose. It's not an accident and you are not the wrong person for the job.

Father, your great plan is amazing. Thank you for giving me my specific grandchildren. Help me to love them well.

HE SEES

Search me, God, and know my heart;
test me and know my anxious thoughts.

Psalm 139:23 NIV

It's a relief to know that we don't even have to figure ourselves out. Even when our own thoughts don't make sense to us, we can call upon the Lord. He can decipher our tangled hearts and anxious thoughts far better than we can. He is trustworthy and good in all that he does. When we cannot do the hard work of managing our emotions, we have a God who is infinitely able.

Each season of life brings new things to navigate. You may expect yourself to have it all figured out by now, but God doesn't. On days when you feel overcome with negativity or worry, lean on God. Be still and let him handle it. Ask him for help and he will help you navigate the things that you don't understand. He is a kind and gentle teacher, who loves to lead his children.

Father, thank you for the security that comes from knowing I am seen by you. Help me to lean on you when I am overwhelmed.

RELY ON OTHERS

Let us consider how we may spur one another on toward love and good deeds.

HEBREWS 10:24 NIV

When Scripture talks about encouraging each other, it is in the context of helping each other stay faithful until the day of Christ's return. We are told to *spur each other on to good deeds* and to keep meeting together while we wait for Jesus to come back. This directive is for the body of Christ as a whole, regardless of age or season of life. God knew that it wouldn't always be easy to wait for Christ's return, but he did equip us with a whole team of people to keep us focused when we are distracted or discouraged.

You can help your children and grandchildren see the great value of being part of a community of believers. You can share with them the blessing other believers have been in your life and the way you've benefited from encouraging others. Show them how you've been lifted up by other believers and how having community has helped you stay on the narrow path.

Father, thank you for the community of believers in my life. Please bless my children and grandchildren with godly friendships.

DISPLAY LOVE

Set a guard, O LORD, over my mouth;
keep watch over the door of my lips!

PSALM 141:3 ESV

Bruises heal and bones can be mended but unkind, careless words can live with a person for years. The way we speak impacts those around us. As believers it should be our desire to speak in a way that honors God and is uplifting of others. This takes discipline and self-control, but God is more than willing to give us both.

As a grandmother, your words matter. The way you speak to your grandchildren will be remembered. Ask God to give you wisdom and discernment in the way that you speak. If you ask, he will help you to guard your lips. Let your speech be kind, gracious, and gentle.

Father, help me to guard my mouth. I don't want to hurt my family with my words. Teach me how to display your love with what I say.

STEER CLEAR

Guide me away from temptation and doing evil.
Save me from sinful habits and from keeping company
with those who are experts in evil.
Help me not to share in their sin in any way!

Psalm 141:4 TPT

The longer we follow God, the more we realize that success does not come from our ability to withstand temptation but in the wisdom to avoid it and the humility to embrace repentance. Scripture continuously warns us to stay away from things that will cause us to sin. God will give us the strength to resist temptation when it arises, but we are also meant to use wisdom and steer clear of it in the first place.

New believers, like your grandchildren, sometimes struggle with this concept. It's not uncommon for people to get themselves into unwise situations because they think they'll be strong enough to handle it. When this happens, encourage your grandchildren to embrace the wisdom of avoiding evil. Remind them that they aren't supposed to rely on their own strength.

Father, help me to continue to avoid sin. Keep my heart soft and help me wisely steer clear of evil.

MORE THAN KNOWING

Although they knew God, they neither glorified him as God nor gave thanks to him, but their thinking became futile and their foolish hearts were darkened.

ROMANS 1:21 NIV

Scripture is clear, we can know God full well and yet still reject him. This tells us that alone, the pursuit of knowledge is not enough. We can have answers to all our questions and still turn away from the Lord. What we know must be translated into a life that glorifies him and continuously gives thanks. Otherwise, even the most knowledgeable will not have faith that lasts.

It's normal for young believers to have a thirst for knowledge. They want everything to be perfectly explained, and they want answers to all their questions. As someone with more experience, you can encourage the young people in your life to value the habit of praise and thanksgiving as much as the pursuit of knowledge. This is what will give their faith longevity.

Father, fill my heart with thanksgiving. I want to always be aware of your greatness and all you've done for me.

AS THE DEER

I lift my hands to you in prayer.
As a dry land needs rain, I thirst for you.

PSALM 143:6 NCV

Sometimes, when we've followed the Lord for a while, our relationship with him becomes habitual and maybe even mundane. As we get older and wiser, we lose some of the passion and zeal we had in our younger years. This isn't necessarily a bad thing, but we do want to be wary of a waning desire for the Lord. His presence is meant to be the thing we seek wholeheartedly for all our days.

If you are feeling tired, ask God to renew your affections for him. As you seek him, he will fill you with a longing for more of his presence. If your time with him has become more of a habit or something you check off a list, ask him for a revitalization of your faith. It is never too late to seek him with the fervor of a new believer.

Father, fill my heart with desire for you. Give me a fresh longing for your presence.

FRESH BEGINNINGS

Tell me in the morning about your love,
because I trust you.
Show me what I should do,
because my prayers go up to you.

Psalm 143:8 NCV

It is good to have a purposeful, regular time with God. When we spend time in prayer each morning, we set the tone for the rest of our day. It gives us an opportunity to eagerly anticipate the sound of his voice. We can then greet the day with confidence in our hearts and excitement to share his goodness with those around us.

Do you look to God each day for guidance? If the answer is no, remember that God waits for you graciously. Don't be discouraged or dismayed by your own weaknesses. He is delighted by your desire to spend time with him and will never greet you with shame when you go to him. He isn't mad at you for not coming sooner, or grouchy that you aren't consistent. He is always merciful and always kind.

Father, help me faithfully meet you every morning. I want to prioritize my time with you.

FAITHFUL LOVE

Who is a God like you, pardoning iniquity
and passing over transgression
for the remnant of his inheritance?
He does not retain his anger forever,
because he delights in steadfast love.

MICAH 7:18 ESV

There is no god like the one we serve. He is the only one who offers the forgiveness of our sins even though we remain undeserving. He loves to be faithful to his children. It is his great delight to keep his promises and lavish us with love. If we want to love like he does, we can seek to treat others in the same way. When we are quick to forgive and slow to anger, we embody his character.

Sometimes it is easy to love our children and grandchildren extravagantly. It seems natural, simple, and effortless. There will surely be seasons when this isn't the case. Sometimes, people are difficult to love. In times when you feel like you can't muster up the right feelings toward your family, seek the Lord. Ask him to give you his perspective and to fill you with the love that he has for them.

God, thank you that you are slow to anger and quick to love. I want to love others in the same way.

TELL YOUR STORY

Let each generation tell its children of your mighty acts;
let them proclaim your power.

PSALM 145:4 NLT

We can all attest to God's faithfulness in different ways. We are meant to share our stories. It can be easy to fall into the trap of thinking that your life experience doesn't matter. The truth is that it is invaluable. The ways that God has shown up for you, both big and small, are monumental and speak to his goodness and reliability.

Don't be shy! Tell your children and grandchildren what God has done. Share with them all the ways that he has been faithful in your life and in the lives of those around you. Proclaim his good deeds and show how he has protected you all your days. You don't have to be swimming in biblical knowledge to give testimony of what God has done in your own life. The way that God has led you is worth sharing with your family. Your story will impact them more than any direction or instruction you could ever give.

Father, give me the courage to share my story with others. I want to testify to your faithfulness.

CONSTANT ADORATION

The LORD is gracious and compassionate,
slow to anger and rich in love.

PSALM 145:8 NIV

God is slow to anger. He is steady, surefooted, and patient beyond what we can understand.

Even when we deserve anger and judgement, he is faithful to forgive us and show us how much he loves us. Each day, without fail, he delights in his children and showers us with blessings.

As a grandmother, you can display this aspect of God's love to your grandchildren. When they make mistakes, you can welcome them with kindness and mercy rather than judgement and annoyance. It's never easy to watch your loved ones make poor decisions but it does allow you the opportunity to love them the way that God does.

Lord, help me to love my grandchildren the way you love me. Help me to show them mercy and kindness even when it's difficult.

HE EQUIPS

May the God of peace who brought again from the dead our Lord Jesus, the great shepherd of the sheep, by the blood of the eternal covenant, equip you with everything good that you may do his will, working in us that which is pleasing in his sight.

HEBREWS 13:20-21 ESV

There is no greater goal in life than to bring glory and honor to God. If we feel that we don't have what it takes to do this well, Scripture explains clearly that God is fully capable of equipping us with everything we need. When we feel insecure, it is good to remember that our opinions of ourselves are not as important as God's. If he says that we can do something, then who are we to doubt.

As you watch your grandchildren grow, you will surely see them stumble and fall. In those moments, remind them that God's strength is far more important than their weaknesses. As they mature God will surely refine them. Yet, even on their best day, they will still be in desperate need of his guidance and power.

Jesus, help me to remember my constant need for you. Help me to teach my children that you are always faithful to equip us.

ONLY GOD

Don't put your confidence in powerful people;
there is no help for you there.

PSALM 146:3 NLT

We all have people we put up on a pedestal. Whether it's a celebrity, a pastor, a friend, or an athlete, we assume they have everything figured out. We proclaim all the good things they've done, and we admire their accomplishments. Truly, this type of thinking sets us up for failure. No human is beyond the ability of great sin. Our greatest admiration should be reserved for God alone, the only one who is absolutely perfect.

The older we get, the less we idolize other people but it's a common occurrence in young people. Encourage your grandchildren to be careful where they place their admiration. Remind them that it's good to have role models but that their confidence should be firmly in the Lord. When their heroes fail, and most will, the state of their heart is revealed.

Father, help my grandchildren not to fall into the trap of idolatry. May their affections be only for you.

NOVEMBER

He gives strength to the faint
and strengthens the powerless.

Isaiah 40:29 CSB

GOOD DIFFERENCES

Each of us has one body with many members, and these members do not all have the same function, so in Christ we, though many, form one body, and each member belongs to all the others. We have different gifts, according to the grace given to each of us.

Romans 12:4-6 NIV

No two people are exactly the same. We each have different personalities, gifts, and weaknesses. We each bring something different to the table. The body of Christ operates best when we value each other without comparison. Unity is found when we embrace that it's okay for us to each play different roles.

As a grandmother, you can recognize and affirm the unique role that your grandchildren will play in this world. Call out the goodness of God in them and encourage them to faithfully tend to their gifts. Give them the freedom to be who God created them to be even if it's different than you expected or doesn't look like you or your children.

Father, help me to value each member of your body. Thank you for making each of us so unique and beautiful.

THE LORD PROTECTS

The LORD protects the foreigners among us.
He cares for the orphans and widows,
but he frustrates the plans of the wicked.

PSALM 146:9 NLT

What a gracious heavenly Father we serve! He is not a tyrant waiting to lower the hammer. He protects those who are oppressed, displaced, and vulnerable. His heart is for the weakest members of society, and his concern is for the defenseless. If he is on the side of the oppressed, then we should be too.

Whether you are aware or not, the children in your life are listening to what you say. They often pick up on nuances that we assume go over their heads. They are observant and learn from what you say and do. If you speak disparagingly about weaker members of society, they will learn to do the same. If you highly value those who are weak and vulnerable, they will learn to do the same. This is not meant to be a reprimand, but a call to live honorably before the young people in your life.

Father, I know that you lift up those who are lowly. Help me to do the same.

LOVE AND REDEMPTION

He heals the wounds of every shattered heart.

Psalm 147:3 TPT

Our heavenly Father meticulously heals every broken heart. He is an expert at it. He smooths over the cracked edges of condemnation. He softens the hardened parts of our hearts. His words of love and redemption regenerate damaged souls and restore them to the joy of his salvation. He is gentle, and his desire is that we are whole and complete in him. He wants only the best for his children.

No matter how your heart has been broken, God is capable of healing it. Maybe you don't have the relationship with your family that you'd hoped for. Maybe you live far away from your grandchildren and are crushed by the distance. Maybe you're grieving a loss or are just struggling to navigate this season of life. No matter the reason, God can take your wounds, bring comfort, and heal them.

Father, please take the pieces of my broken heart, and make it whole.

KNOWLEDGE OF LOVE

This is my prayer for you: that your love will grow more and more; that you will have knowledge and understanding with your love; that you will see the difference between good and bad and will choose the good; that you will be pure and without wrong for the coming of Christ.

PHILIPPIANS 1:9-10 NCV

As Paul prayed for the Philippian church to be Christlike, he did not pray that they would try harder, do better, or be more successful. His greatest hope was that they would have a greater knowledge of God's love. He knew that if that was their foundation, that everything else would follow.

You are not meant to have a checklist that determines your success with the Lord. Your belonging is not determined by your ability to pray, have consistent quiet times, and say or do the right things. You are accepted based on the sacrifice of Jesus. His love and selflessness are what allows you to be near to God. His extravagant love should be the greatest pursuit of your life.

Father, help me to grow in the knowledge of your love. I know that it is my strong foundation.

FEAR THE LORD

The Lord delights in those who fear him,
who put their hope in his unfailing love.

Psalm 147:11 NIV

God is fully aware of our humanity. He knows that we are prone to wander and are easily distracted. He isn't dismayed by our short attention span or fed up with our inability to do the right thing. His delight does not come from our great skills or how impressive we are. His delight comes from those who fear him.

When you fear the Lord, you respect him. This means that you are aware of his great strength and your great weakness. Fear of the Lord cannot come from boasting about your own goodness. It comes from humility and the acceptance of your frailty. As you embrace your weakness and lean on God's strength, your family will see what it looks like to live a faith filled life.

Thank you, Father, for the great love you have shown me. Help me to be reverent toward you.

READ AND APPLY

Anyone who listens to the word but does not do what it says is like someone who looks at his face in a mirror and, after looking at himself, goes away and immediately forgets what he looks like.

James 1:23-24 NIV

When we read God's Word and neglect to apply it to our lives, we miss the point. We set ourselves up for failure when we don't utilize the resources that God has so abundantly given us. All of Scripture is valuable and applicable. There aren't any trials, decisions, or temptations that cannot be navigated with the help of God's Word.

You could spend your whole life reading the Word without applying any of it to your life. It's not meant to just be read; it's meant to be utilized. Don't be overwhelmed by the magnitude of this. You aren't expected to apply the entire Bible to your life at once. Simply ask the Holy Spirit for direction. He will faithfully and gently reveal to you what you need to focus on.

God, help me hide your Word in my heart. Teach me how to apply it to my life daily.

CONSTANT PRAISE

Let everything that has breath
praise the LORD.
Praise the LORD.

PSALM 150:6 ESV

When we read the garden account in Genesis, we get a little glimpse of what life was intended to look like. All of creation existed harmoniously, communing with the Lord, and praising him continuously. This is how we are meant to operate. Every single part of creation is meant to praise the Lord.

One day, Jesus will come back, and everything will return to the way it was supposed to be at the beginning. You will spend eternity praising the Lord. All of creation will be free of conflict, death, and pain. Let your heart be filled with hope as you anticipate that day. For as many days as breath fills your lungs, praise the Lord with all you have.

Father, help me to develop the habit of constant praise. You are so worthy!

SLOW TO ANGER

Everyone should be quick to listen, slow to speak and slow to become angry, because human anger does not produce the righteousness that God desires.

JAMES 1:19-20 NIV

We are not meant to act out in anger. No matter what excuse we come up with, the Bible is clear; angry actions do not accomplish what God wants. We might think that we are right, but the better reaction would be to quiet our hearts and listen. This takes self-control and is a skill that can be practiced little by little. We won't wake up one day and have complete control over our emotions. Instead, little by little we can change our habits.

If you grew up in an angry household or were an angry parent yourself, you might feel defeated at the mention of self-control. You don't have to be an angry grandparent. It is never too late to learn new habits and seek restoration. God does not intend for his children to consistently boil over in emotion. Ask him for wisdom and let him gently lead you down a different path. If your desire is to be slow to anger, he will faithfully help you.

Father, I want my anger to be subject to you. Help me to have self-control and to manage my emotions well.

DESIRE OBEDIENCE

Live as God's obedient children. Don't slip back into your old ways of living to satisfy your own desires. You didn't know any better then. But now you must be holy in everything you do, just as God who chose you is holy.

1 Peter 1:14-15 NLT

We've all watched our grandchildren do the same naughty thing over and over. They've been told no, they realize they are wrong, yet they continue to do exactly what they want. It's almost amusing to watch small children behave this way. They can be persistent in their naughtiness. We chuckle but do we realize that we often do the exact same thing?

Have you ever continued to do something even though you knew it was wrong? If you think about it, you can surely come up with a habit in your life that could use improvement. Even as a mature adult, you still sometimes seek to satisfy your own desires. This isn't a behavior that is limited to children. When you find yourself in that situation, remember that God has given you everything you need to live a holy life. He has fully equipped you to live in a way that honors him.

Father, lead me on the narrow road. Help me to be obedient to all that you ask of me.

NARROW PATH

Blessed is the one who does not walk in step with the wicked
or stand in the way that sinners take
or sit in the company of mockers,
but whose delight is in the law of the LORD.

PSALM 1:1-2 NIV

Children whose main goal is to be cool often end up in situations they didn't anticipate. The desire to fit in can cause them to make choices they wouldn't otherwise. They are desperate to belong and so they bend and compromise their standards in ways they never thought they would. Instead of walking the narrow path, they allow their desire for acceptance to control their actions.

As a grandparent, you have the privilege of instilling a steady sense of belonging in the hearts of your grandchildren. That's not to say that you alone will prevent them from succumbing to peer pressure, but you can certainly play a role. Teach them of their unshakeable identity in Christ and speak truth over them every chance you get. Let your faithful love remind them of the faithful love of their creator.

God, help my grandchildren to be faithful to you. Assure them of their belonging and keep them away from wickedness.

TRIALS

When troubles of any kind come your way, consider it an opportunity for great joy. For you know that when your faith is tested, your endurance has a chance to grow.

JAMES 1:2-3 NLT

Trials allow the Lord to do the deepest work in our hearts. Challenges draw us to our knees, giving God the opportunity to transform us into the likeness of his Son. We so badly want to avoid difficult days, yet when we look back at the spiritual growth and the increase in our faith, we wouldn't trade them for anything.

The trials that you face in this season of your life are different from what you would have faced in your younger years. Trust that while your season of life is different, God's ability to help you navigate it is the same. You can still trust him to help you mature. He is the same faithful God who has been with you all your days.

Jesus, I rejoice in your work in me. Help me to face trials with courage and confidence, knowing that you are always with me.

GREAT PLEASURE

The LORD takes pleasure in his people;
he adorns the humble with salvation.

PSALM 149:4 CSB

We get so much joy from seeing the precious faces of our grandchildren. Their sweetness and excitement when they run to us is thrilling. That purity and love gives us some insight into how God feels about us. He adores his children. He looks forward to spending time with us and is delighted by our glance.

God takes great pleasure in you. You bring joy to his heart and a smile to his face. He looks at you with pride and adoration. You are his precious creation, made in his image and full of his glory. You wouldn't hesitate to say that the children in your life are precious to God. Remember that you are his child, and he is delighted by you.

God, thank you for the way that you delight in me. Help me to further understand your love.

HONOR THEM

Listen to your father's teaching
and do not forget your mother's advice.
Their teaching will be like flowers in your hair
or a necklace around your neck.

PROVERBS 1:8-9 NCV

It is good to encourage our grandchildren to honor their parents. When we witness them obeying their parents, we can tell them how proud we are of them. It's good to let them know that they are also pleasing God. We can remind our grandkids that the Lord has entrusted them to their mom and dad specifically. He chose this particular family for them because he knew what was best. God is glorified when they listen to and obey their parents.

We can support our children by honoring the authority that they have in their children's life. The relationship they have with their children is more important than ours. While we adore our grandchildren, our highest goal should be to see them thrive with their parents, not just with us.

Father, I lift up my children and grandchildren to you. May their relationship honor you and bring you joy.

HOW GREAT

Great is our Lord, and abundant in power;
his understanding is beyond measure.

Psalm 147:5 ESV

God's understanding is beyond any other. His knowledge is so vast that we can't begin to grasp it. There is nothing that he doesn't understand. There is no trial that we can face, no complicated relationship, no miscommunication that is too messy or confusing for God. Where our minds are limited, his is limitless. When we are stumped, annoyed, frustrated, or confused, we can turn to him for guidance. It would be foolish not to.

When you face a problem, do you utilize the resources available to you? When you ask God for help you acknowledge his great ability. Not only is he capable, but he is also willing. He loves it when you turn to him, trusting in his ways over your own.

Father, help me to run to you when I need help. I know that there is nothing your power cannot accomplish.

FAITHFUL FATHER

The Lord is like a father to his children,
tender and compassionate to those who fear him.
For he knows how weak we are;
he remembers we are only dust.

Psalm 103:13-14 NLT

The Lord knows our frailties. He sees our weaknesses fully and loves us extravagantly. He is gentle toward us because he knows that we are limited in our strength and understanding. This is how we are meant to behave toward those who are weaker than we are. We are supposed to be gentle and kind, never taking advantage of the disadvantages of other people.

Your gentleness toward your grandchildren reflects God's gentleness toward you. The way that you value them, encourage them, and cherish them speaks of God's tender love. He lifts up the lowly and protects the weak. He is a good and faithful father.

Father, thank you for your great love. I want to love others in the compassionate way that you love me.

CLEAR DIRECTIVE

"'Love the Lord your God with all your heart and with all your soul and with all your mind and with all your strength.' The second is this: 'Love your neighbor as yourself.' There is no commandment greater than these."

MARK 12:30-31 NIV

We often overcomplicate God's will. We fret and wonder if we've missed our calling or if we've made the right choices. If we look to Scripture God's will for our lives can be summed up by loving him and loving our neighbors. If those two things are our priority, then we can rest assured that we are firmly following the right path.

There is no need to overcomplicate it. All that he asks is for you to follow the command found in Mark. Loving God and your neighbor can be done anytime, anyplace, and in any season of your life. It's never too late and you haven't missed the boat. No matter what the focus of your life has been, your highest goal should be to follow those commands well.

Father, help me to love and others well. When I get distracted, remind me that this is the most important instruction you've given me.

ALL GENERATIONS

Your faithfulness endures to all generations;
you have established the earth, and it stands fast.

PSALM 119:90 ESV

We have a heavenly King who never fails us. He will always come through and he is never late. Everything he has pre-ordained will go according to plan, and no man can change it. The future is set in stone. His plans and his character are dependable, steady, and unchanging.

God has faithfully led each generation before you. He has steadily walked with you and has protected you well. He will do the same for your children and grandchildren. Your life is a testimony to his goodness and theirs will be too. His faithfulness didn't start with you, and it does not end with you. You are part of a glorious story that is perfectly interwoven and testifies to the glory of God.

Father, thank you for your steadfast faithfulness. Thank you for being unchanging and dependable.

TURN TO SCRIPTURE

Oh, how I love your law!
I meditate on it all day long.

PSALM 119:97 NIV

God's Word is available to us for instruction, guidance, and encouragement. We can wake up every morning and read about how to handle whatever challenge we are facing. When we hide God's Word in our hearts, we will find ourselves leaning on his understanding over our own. When trials arise, we are already well equipped to handle them.

You have all the tools you need to navigate the grandparenting years of your life. Even as you face new challenges or circumstances you didn't expect, God's Word is just as poignant as it has always been. As you face changes in your career, turn to Scripture. As you help your children to be Godly parents, turn to Scripture. As the seasons of your marriage change, turn to Scripture. No matter what you face, hiding the Word in your heart will equip you well.

Father, help me hide your Word in my heart. I'm so thankful for your instructions and encouragement.

TRUE LIGHT

Your word is a lamp to guide my feet
and a light for my path.

Psalm 119:105 NLT

We pray that our grandchildren will stay on the narrow path. We want them to follow Jesus and to avoid the pitfalls of sin. It can be scary watching them try to navigate today's culture. Everything is so different from when we were parents. The best and most faithful resource that they have is the Word of God. Even though culture has shifted drastically, God's Word remains the same.

Pray that your grandchildren will grow in affection for the Word. If they love God's Word, they won't look elsewhere for insight. Pray that God would fill them with a desire for knowledge and that they would turn to Scripture for understanding. Study the Word so that you can guide them in truth and disciple them well.

Jesus, give my grandchildren a hunger for your Word. Equip them to follow you well.

GREAT AFFECTION

The LORD opens the eyes of the blind.
The LORD lifts up those who are weighed down.
The LORD loves the godly.

PSALM 146:8 NLT

When we look at examples of what God has done, we see that he cares tenderly for those who might feel overlooked. He pays attention to those who feel ignored, left behind, or even useless. He doesn't brush past the problems that his children face. He is aware of them all, and he is faithful to heal, redeem, and comfort.

God sees you exactly where you are. He sees the way that you laid your life down for your children in your mothering years. He sees the way that you continue to lay your life down as the matriarch of your family. He sees how hard you work. He is just as aware of you now as he was when you were the one with a baby on your hip. You are still now, and will forever be, his precious child who he sees with great tenderness.

Father, thank you for seeing me. I am thankful for your loving kindness.

DIFFERENT GIFTS

If your gift is serving others, serve them well. If you are a teacher, teach well. If your gift is to encourage others, be encouraging. If it is giving, give generously. If God has given you leadership ability, take the responsibility seriously. And if you have a gift for showing kindness to others, do it gladly.

ROMANS 12:7-8 NLT

We each have different gifts and are expected to utilize them well. While we should work hard within our gifts, we should also be respectful of the gifts of others. We aren't meant to compare ourselves to each other or take over and manage everything on our own. We are meant to work collaboratively, striving toward unity and harmony in the body of Christ.

As parents, your children will have different strengths and weaknesses than you. They will thrive in areas where you failed, and they will flounder in areas that were easy for you. Their gifts are different from yours. Let your words be gracious and life giving, admiring the way that God has gifted each of them.

Father, thank you for the many gifts you have given. Help me to value all of them.

EVER-PRESENT

My help comes from the LORD,
who made heaven and earth!

PSALM 121:2 NLT

God is attentive to our cries and comes to our aid when we need him. His ears are turned in our direction. His eyes are always on us. We don't have to fear trials or wonder how we will get through life. The creator of the entire universe leads us faithfully through it. What more could we possibly want?

When you need help, where do you turn? In every circumstance God should be the one you consult first. He is waiting for you to reach out and lean on his strength. He is readily available to you. There is nothing you can face that is too difficult for him to manage. You don't ever need to be embarrassed or ashamed of asking him for help. If he can intricately weave together all of creation, he can surely help you navigate your life.

God, thank you for being my ever-present help. I know that you are always there when I need you.

CONSISTENCY

Behave decently, as in the daytime, not in carousing and drunkenness, not in sexual immorality and debauchery, not in dissension and jealousy. Rather, clothe yourselves with the Lord Jesus Christ, and do not think about how to gratify the desires of the flesh.

Romans 13:13-14 NIV

We have all heard the cautionary tale of someone behaving one way on Sunday and differently the rest of the week. It's important to search our own hearts to make sure that we are consistent in the way that we behave. Do we change our demeanors based on who we are with?

The way that you behave when you think no one is paying attention reveals the true state of your heart. Ask the Holy Spirit to show you if there are areas in your lift that don't align with scripture. He will faithfully reveal to you where repentance is needed. His voice is gentle, peaceful, and always points you to truth. Listen with humility and seek to live in a way that honors the Lord.

Jesus, help me to live authentically for you. I don't want to have duplicity in my life.

ALWAYS NEAR

The LORD is near to all who call on him,
to all who call on him in truth.

PSALM 145:18 NIV

God always hears when we call. He promises that he is close to us, and he always sticks to his Word. If we feel far from him, it's important to focus on the truth instead of our emotions. Scripture promises that he is near, and we can trust what Scripture says.

Young people especially have seasons when they are convinced God is far from them. It takes maturity to be able to believe the truth instead of relying on how you feel. When your grandchildren are discouraged, remind them of what the Word says. As they grow, they will find security and steadfastness in what God says is true.

God, give my grandchildren an unshakable belief that you are near. May they never doubt that you are close when they call.

NO RECORDS

Love is patient, love is kind. Love does not envy,
is not boastful, is not arrogant, is not rude, is not self-seeking,
is not irritable, and does not keep a record of wrongs.

1 Corinthians 13:4-5 CSB

It's easy to keep a mental record of wrongs without realizing it. We think we've forgiven the issue, but it keeps coming up in our minds. We dwell on what was done to us and the person who did it. We find ourselves making rude comments in our minds as we ruminate on how there should be consequences.

This type of behavior does not reflect God's love. Just like God does not keep track of our transgressions, we are not supposed to keep track of our offenses. If you've noticed yourself making a list of wrongs, ask God to help you. Ask him to give you compassion and empathy toward the other person. He will soften your heart and help you to extend true grace.

Jesus, help me love as you do, sacrificially and unconditionally, without keeping a record of wrongs.

WONDERFULLY MADE

You created my inmost being;
you knit me together in my mother's womb.
I praise you because I am fearfully and wonderfully made;
your works are wonderful,
I know that full well.

PSALM 139:13-14 NIV

Every child, regardless of how they enter a family, is precious in God's sight. They are meant to be exactly where he places them. He oversaw the development of every cell, every bone, and each organ. He gave gifts and created individual personalities. In his wisdom he decided what they would do and where they would live.

It's such a joy to have grandchildren in your life. Grandparenting is an honor and a blessing. You get to teach your grandchildren how precious, lovely, and delightful they are. Remind them that God created them on purpose. They are his masterpiece, and he adores them.

Father, thank you for my grandchildren who are made in your image! Help them to know how beloved they are.

OTHERS FIRST

We who are strong ought to bear with the failings of the weak and not to please ourselves. Each of us should please our neighbors for their good, to build them up.

ROMANS 15:1-2 NIV

Children typically consider themselves first. We've all seen them clammer for the first slice of cake, the front seat of the car, or their choice for family movie night. We are all born with a tendency to put our desires first. It takes practice and intentionality to think about what other people want and need.

Children aren't the only selfish ones. Even as a grown adult, you might still have areas in your life that are defined by selfishness. Instead of seeking to please your neighbor, you might come up with all kinds of reasons why your needs or wants are more important. Today, ask God how you can grow in this area. Trust his tender leadership and expand your capacity to love others.

Father, I want to be thoughtful and generous toward my neighbors. Help me see areas where I can improve.

HIGHER WAYS

"Even dogs eat the scraps beneath their masters' table."
"Dear woman," Jesus said to her, "your faith is great.
Your request is granted."
And her daughter was instantly healed.

MATTHEW 15:27-28 NLT

The woman in today's verse approached Jesus and asked him to have mercy on her daughter who was oppressed by a demon. The disciples begged him to send her away because her begging was bothering them. In his graciousness, Jesus ended up healing her child. Jesus doesn't operate based on the opinions of others.

This woman was bothersome, persistent, and considered less than. According to the disciples, Jesus had every reason to ignore her request and send her away. He didn't follow the rules of man then and he doesn't now. His work in your life might look the way you think it should. Remember that it's not his job to operate based off our preconceived notions. His ways are above ours.

Lord, thank you for being so merciful. Increase my faith and help me to trust in you for big things.

STAY SOFT

Those who accept correction gain understanding.
Respect for the LORD will teach you wisdom.
If you want to be honored, you must be humble.

PROVERBS 15:32–33 NCV

When we stay open to the work of the Holy Spirit, we show the Lord that we want growth in our lives. Our willingness to accept correction relates directly to how much wisdom we have. If we stubbornly remain where we are we will miss out on the abundant life that God intends for us. We dislike correction to our own detriment.

As you get older, fight to keep your heart soft. Be open to the correction of the Lord and learn to love growth. Don't give in to the stereotype that you must be stubborn or set in your ways as you age. Trust that any urging of the Holy Spirit to change comes from love and an understanding of what is best for you.

Father, I humble myself, accept your discipline, and ask you to keep my heart soft.

FORGIVENESS

"Lord, how many times shall by brother sin against me and I still forgive him? Up to seven times?" Jesus said to him, "I do not say to you, up to seven times, but up to seventy-seven times."

MATTHEW 18:21-22 NASB

Forgiveness is not always easy. It can be difficult, laborious, and humbling. Sometimes It takes serious effort to forgive a wrong that we would rather cling to. Left to our own devices, we would rather hold onto offenses and be justified in our hurt or frustration. It's not easy to forgive but it is the way of Christ. We are meant to forgive because we have been forgiven.

There is so much debate over what true forgiveness looks like. The best approach is to embrace humility and be led by the Holy Spirit. If you are soft hearted, he will be faithful to bring conviction when it's needed. As you follow him, he won't lead you down the wrong path. Trust the truth of scripture of the urging of the Holy Spirit in your life.

Holy Spirit, keep my heart soft. Help me to forgive others readily and with humility, knowing that I have been forgiven.

DECEMBER

I will cause your name to be remembered for all generations; Therefore the peoples will praise you forever and ever.

Psalm 45:17 CSB

COMPLAINING

Do everything without complaining and arguing, so that no one can criticize you. Live clean, innocent lives as children of God, shining like bright lights in a world full of crooked and perverse people.

PHILIPPIANS 2:14-15 NLT

Complaining and arguing isn't limited to children. When we picture these traits we might think of whining, temper tantrums, and other childlike behavior. The truth is that plenty of adults never grow out of this way of living. The world is filled with people who constantly complain, spread negativity, and insist on being right. None of these things are honoring to God.

Are you stuck in a pattern of complaint? When you are inconvenienced do you handle it with grace, or do you tell the first person you talk to how miserable you are? Negative habits have a way of sneaking into our lives without us realizing how prevalent they are. If you ask the Holy Spirit, he will gently point out areas in your life that need redirection. Trust his guidance and humbly repent.

God, help me to be aware of complaint in my life. I don't want to be a negative person who is constantly whining.

INTERESTS OF OTHERS

Don't look out only for your own interests,
but take an interest in others, too.

PHILIPPIANS 2:4 NLT

We are meant to care about the people around us more than we care for ourselves. When the body of Christ does this well, each person's needs are met. When we care for each other adequately, no one is left wanting. In a society that idolizes self-care, godly selflessness is radical.

As a grandmother, you have plenty of opportunities to put the interests of others before your own. Caring for children isn't usually convenient. It inherently takes sacrifice and selflessness. Furthermore, you can look at the interests of your grown children. What do they need from you in this season of life? What they need from you might not look the way you want it too. This is an opportunity to look out for the interests of others above your own.

Jesus, help me to love others sacrificially. I want to put the interests of others above my own.

YOUR DAUGHTERS

Teach the young women to love their husbands,
to love their children, to be wise and pure,
to be good workers at home, to be kind.

TITUS 2:4-5 NCV

It can be tempting to view grandparenting as a reward for having done the work of parenting yourself. Many people see this season as a fun time after years of hard work. While grandchildren are certainly a reward to be cherished, our work as mothers is not over. We have been told in Scripture to disciple the next generation. We have the privilege of teaching our daughters how to be wives and mothers.

You are desperately and vitally needed. Your role as a mother is not over, it's simply shifting. You have the privilege of passing on the mantle of godly mothering. You can encourage and support your daughters as they seek to be God honoring wives and mothers. Your role in this season is so much more than just enjoying your grandkids and then sending them back home.

Father, thank you for this season of life. Help me to love my daughters well.

TEACH THEM

Encourage the young men to be self-controlled. In everything set them an example by doing what is good. In your teaching show integrity, seriousness and soundness of speech that cannot be condemned.

Titus 2:6-8 NIV

As our sons become fathers, it is our job as the older generation to teach them how to embrace self-control and integrity. For us to do this well, we must embody those qualities ourselves. We must embrace humility and show our adult children that we are a trustworthy source of wisdom. Our job is not to give them our opinions but to faithfully point them to Jesus.

As a grandmother, the best way you can influence your family is by setting a good example and glorifying God above yourself. Scripture clearly outlines how important it is for young men and women to be discipled by those who are older than them. They are in the throws of some of life's biggest challenges and hopefully they will look to you for wisdom.

Father, help me to instruct my adult children well. I want to point them to you more than I want them to listen to my opinion.

GREAT EQUALIZER

It is by grace you have been saved, through faith—and this is not from yourselves, it is the gift of God—not by works, so that no one can boast.

Ephesians 2:8-9 NIV

God understands our propensity to take credit for what is good. We all love to have good things attributed to us. We love to be flattered, noticed, and adored. The gospel is the great equalizer. There is not, nor will there ever be, a human who can take any credit for its goodness. No one can claim the idea or say that their hard work made it come to pass. We are all equally inadequate before the cross.

A lifetime of good work still doesn't add up to salvation. There is nothing that you can do to earn what you've been freely given. When you remember this, you will find yourself much more likely to embrace humility and be gracious toward others. Today, ask God to give you a fresh revelation of the simple gospel.

Father, thank you for the greatest gift of all—your precious Son. Thank you for the humility that the cross requires.

CHASING WEALTH

Don't wear yourself out trying to get rich;
be wise enough to control yourself.
Wealth can vanish in the wink of an eye.

PROVERBS 23:4-5 NCV

While Scripture warns us to use wisdom in managing our finances, it also warns blatantly against idolizing riches. We are not meant to wear ourselves thin trying to chase after worldly treasures. Even if we diligently plan and carefully save, money can disappear in an instant. It is not the most important thing, and we shouldn't treat it as such.

Maybe you've experienced hardship and are not where you thought you would be financially at this point in your life. Maybe you've prioritized wealth and have achieved great success. Either way, money is not supposed to be your primary concern in this life. Take a moment and ask yourself if you've given wealth, or the idea of wealth, more space in your heart than it should have.

Father, you are my first love above everything else. Help me not to idolize riches.

ASK FOR WISDOM

Through wisdom a house is built,
and by understanding it is established;
by knowledge the rooms are filled
with all precious and pleasant riches.
A wise man is strong,
Yes, a man of knowledge increases strength.

PROVERBS 24:3-5 NKJV

When we pray for our grandchildren, wisdom should be at the top of our list. Wisdom is the firm foundation of a life that honors the Lord. If they are wise our children and grandchildren will make decisions that please the Lord. They will find blessings and favor and they will be a benefit to everyone around them.

When you pray for your family, what are your highest hopes for them? Do you focus on their happiness, protection, or circumstances? Scripture says that wisdom is the starting point for all of these things. Above anything else you might want for them, ask God to give them an abundance of wisdom.

Father, please give my grandchildren wisdom. Give them a thirst for knowledge and understanding.

HANDS AND FEET

"I was hungry and you gave me something to eat,
I was thirsty and you gave me something to drink,
I was a stranger and you invited me in, I needed clothes
and you clothed me, I was sick and you looked after me,
I was in prison and you came to visit me."

MATTHEW 25:35-36 NIV

We are the hands and feet of Jesus. Our words and actions can display the character of Christ for everyone we meet. We are called to live a life of service for the good of others. Whatever we do for others, we do for Christ. This is a high and glorious calling. The Son of Man laid his life down for us and we can honor him in the way that we lay our lives down for others.

It's easy to look at the lowly or the wicked and see their need for Jesus. Sometimes we forget that our own families are just as vital and important. You can honor God by serving your family well. You can be obedient to the calling of Christ by loving your children and grandchildren with kindness and generosity. There is no difference between the ministry of loving your family and the ministry of loving the lowly.

Jesus, help me be your hands and feet. I want to glorify you in the way that I love my family.

PEACEABLE AND GENTLE

Remind the people to be subject to rulers and authorities,
to be obedient, to be ready to do whatever is good,
to slander no one, to be peaceable and considerate,
and always to be gentle toward everyone.

TITUS 3:1-2 NIV

Titus is clear about behavior that honors the Lord. If we measure general society against it, we'll see that many fall short. How many of us love to speak poorly about our leaders and authorities? We want our opinions to be known, especially if we disagree with how someone behaves or the stances that they take.

As a grandmother, you can influence the generation that comes after you. You honor the Lord when you speak gently, peaceably, and considerately about everyone. There are no exceptions to this Scripture. You cannot speak peaceably about the people you agree with while defaming those you don't. Even in disagreement, you can be gracious and kind.

Father, fill me with your Spirit and help me to honor everyone with my words. Teach me how to speak peaceably and graciously.

GRATEFUL AND HAPPY

God wants all people to eat and drink
and be happy in their work,
which are gifts from God.

ECCLESIASTES 3:13 NCV

Our attitudes determine our outlook. Is the glass half full or half empty? There are some people who will never be happy no matter what. Even when God's blessings are evident in their life, they are still always dissatisfied. Truly, this type of attitude gets in the way of the thanksgiving that God deserves from us.

God's desire is not that you would be unhappy and bemoaning the life you have. Surely, the blessings in your life are many. When you choose to compare what you have to others or get caught up in materialism, it's easy to think that nothing is good enough. Instead, ask God to soften your heart and open your eyes to the good things in your life.

Father, forgive me for my ungratefulness. Open my eyes to all the good things in my life.

HIS SOLUTIONS

Trust in the LORD with all your heart;
do not depend on your own understanding.
Seek his will in all you do,
and he will show you which path to take.

PROVERBS 3:5-6 NLT

Our own strategies pale compared to God's solutions. Scripture promises if we trust him and seek him, he'll be faithful. He'll light the path and direct our steps. We need God's way, not our own. His plans are infinitely better than our own. When we look to him, we gain the wisdom of his insight as well as the peace that comes from relinquishing control.

As you navigate the second half of your life, it's never too late to develop the habit of seeking his will in all you do. Each day presents an opportunity to honor him with the choices that you make. These next years may be filled with trials that you have never faced before. Your softness toward Gods voice is just as important now as it's ever been.

Father, I trust your guidance. I want to seek your will in all that I do.

SPEAK LOVINGLY

With the tongue we praise our Lord and Father, and with it we curse human beings, who have been made in God's likeness. Out of the same mouth come praise and cursing. My brothers and sisters, this should not be.

James 3:9-10 NIV

It's easy to read this verse and begin a debate about how we should define the word *curse*. We get caught up in what that could mean and add one more thing to our personal collection of dos and don'ts. If this is how we read scripture, then we are likely missing the point. The main point of this verse is that we are treating other people with the same love and kindness that God does. It's not okay to say we love God, and then speak poorly to his children.

Are you more concerned with vocabulary than you are with cherishing others through conversation? If the answer is yes, perhaps it's time for a heart evaluation. Let God open your eyes to how he sees his children and let that transform the way that you speak.

Jesus, help me display your love in the way that I speak. Teach me how to glorify you with my words.

WISDOM FIRST

My child, listen and accept what I say.
Then you will have a long life.
I am guiding you in the way of wisdom,
and I am leading you on the right path.

PROVERBS 4:10-12 NCV

Solomon, the author of Proverbs, is giving his son a warning about the importance of wisdom. He knew firsthand how pursuing God's wisdom could have a monumental impact. Wisdom was his greatest treasure, and he wanted to pass it on to his son. As grandparents, there are probably many things we wish for the children in our lives. At the top of that list should be the consistent pursuit of wisdom.

When you think about what you want for your grandchildren, what comes to mind? Do you want them to be well behaved, successful, or happy? There is nothing inherently wrong with any of these things, but the pursuit of wisdom should always come first. Scripture is clear about how important it is. There is no greater gift that you can give your grandchildren than the passing on of godly wisdom.

Father, thank you for giving us wisdom so abundantly. Give my grandchildren a desire for wisdom.

ALREADY SATISFIED

I know how to make do with little, and I know how to make do with a lot. In any and all circumstances I have learned the secret of being content—whether well fed or hungry, whether in abundance or in need.

PHILIPPIANS 4:12 CSB

This time of year, it's easy to get lost in the hustle and bustle of consumerism. It's easy to feel the pull for more and more stuff. It's important to take the time to think about the state of our hearts. Are we engaged in generosity or are we more focused on making sure that our holiday season is delightful? We are not meant to gather earthly treasures; our main focus should be elsewhere.

The apostle Paul knew all about living with plenty as well as being in poverty. God allowed both circumstances in his life and Paul learned to be content. He knew that nothing could separate him from Christ. He knew that no matter what else was going on, Christ's love was all he needed.

Father, thank you for the gift of your Son. Help me to be fully satisfied with what you have given me.

TRUE MOTIVES

You do not have because you do not ask. You ask and don't receive because you ask with wrong motives, so that you may spend it on your pleasures.

JAMES 4:2-3 CSB

It's common to read the first part of this Scripture and forget about the rest. We are familiar with the idea that we need to ask to receive but we must also remember that our motives are important. Asking is not the only biblical stipulation for prayers to be answered. Sometimes, God doesn't give us what we want because the motives of our heart are wrong.

If your desire is to honor God, he will be faithful to show you what is in your heart. When he reveals your true motives, respond with humility, and follow his guidance. The more you surrender your thoughts and intentions to him, the more they will align with what is good and right.

Father, show me my motives when they don't align with truth. Help me to be flexible and willing to grow.

IN GOD'S HANDS

Do not worry about anything, but pray and ask God for everything you need, always giving thanks. And God's peace, which is so great we cannot understand it, will keep your hearts and minds in Christ Jesus.

PHILIPPIANS 4:6-7 NCV

When we dwell on our worries, we give them weight and authority in our minds. We worry as though our thoughts will change the outcome of our circumstances. The Bible is clear that worrying cannot accomplish anything. It is best to leave all our problems in God's hands.

Life is so much better when you acknowledge that the God of all creation is really, truly in control. Trusting him with the details of your life brings freedom and peace. When you are tempted to focus on your fears, remember that God simply wants you to ask him for help. There is no reason to be lost in worry or anxiety when God is on your side.

Father, help me to surrender my worries to you. I don't want to be lost in anxiety when I can rely on your strength.

DRAW NEAR

Submit to God. Resist the devil, and he will flee from you. Draw near to God, and he will draw near to you.

JAMES 4:7-8 CSB

Submitting to God is the only way to truly resist the devil. When we are in a close relationship with the God, our minds are on him, his goodness, and his love. We allow the living Word to dwell in our hearts and minds, and we follow the leading of the Holy Spirit. There is no room for Satan in a life that is surrendered to God.

If your mind is filled with worry and fear, take some time to lay it before the Lord. Be deliberate in telling him what you are afraid of. You don't need to organize your thoughts or present him with a list that makes sense. He is big enough to handle your jumbled thoughts and most irrational fears. Invite him into every corner of your heart and mind.

Father, keep me close to you, protected, surrendered, and secure.

DON'T DESPAIR

We are afflicted in every way, but not crushed; perplexed, but not driven to despair; persecuted, but not forsaken; struck down, but not destroyed; always carrying in the body the death of Jesus, so that the life of Jesus may also be manifested in our bodies.

2 Corinthians 4:8-10 ESV

The Bible says very clearly that we will face trials, persecutions, and possibly even death for the cause of Christ. If we surrender to Jesus, we will share in his sufferings. Some will suffer to a greater degree than others. Whatever we face, we know that he will give us his power to endure.

Have you ever felt offended or betrayed by the difficulties in your life? The presence of conflict does not equal a lack of God's presence. He is with you through every trial and hardship. He is close to those who are hurting and is faithful to lead his children. When you are struggling, remember that it is an opportunity to display the life of Jesus.

Jesus, thank you for the privilege of sharing in your sufferings. Help me to see you clearly amid suffering.

BLESS YOUR LEADERS

Honor those who are your leaders in the Lord's work. They work hard among you and give you spiritual guidance. Show them great respect and wholehearted love because of their work. And live peacefully with each other.

1 THESSALONIANS 5:12-13 NLT

We often forget to thank our pastors and church staff for their tireless work. It's easy to criticize how churches function when we aren't the ones doing the work. Instead of pointing out the flaws we see, we should seek to encourage those who are leading us. We should pray earnestly for their families and look for opportunities to bless them.

As an older member of the church, you can be an example for others of how to respect and appreciate leaders. You can be willing to serve them and to honor them. Pay attention to the sacrifices of others and ask God for creative ways to show them how thankful you are. Instead of looking on the decisions of others, ask God to help you graciously support your leaders.

Father, make me sensitive to the needs of church leadership. Help me continually bless them.

IN THE MUNDANE

Rejoice always, pray without ceasing, in everything give thanks; for this is the will of God in Christ Jesus for you.

1 THESSALONIANS 5:16-18 NKJV

Without realizing it, we often read scripture with our own built-in caveats. We read that we should give thanks in all circumstances and then we only apply that to the situations we want to. It takes a lot of mental work to praise God amid confusion, frustration, or conflict. We are not meant to pray only when things are good, or when they are horribly bad. It's usually the everyday frustrations and irritations that are the hardest to surrender to the Lord.

At this point in your life, you've likely experienced great trials and great joy. Those extreme times are when it's easiest to lean on the Lord. Remember that most of your life is spent in the middle, the mundane, and the boring. Today, try communicating with God in normal and typical moments. He wants to share it all with you.

Father, help me rejoice, pray and always be thankful. I don't want my prayers to be limited to extreme situations.

STRONG IN TRIALS

We can rejoice, too, when we run into problems and trials, for we know that they help us develop endurance. And endurance develops strength of character, and character strengthens our confident hope of salvation.

ROMANS 5:3-4 NLT

When we encounter trials, the Holy Spirit strengthens us. When we trust that the Lord won't leave us alone, our faith grows. The more we have trouble, the more we develop perseverance. As we experience new trials, we can gain strength from knowing that God has been faithful in the past and he will be again.

Each difficulty that you face can prepare you for the next one. Even when you don't understand why you are going through something, you can trust that if nothing else, your faith can be strengthened. Steadily, you will grow in faith and hope. As you become familiar with God's ability to help you, leaning on him will be second nature. The more you do it, the easier it becomes.

Father, help me endure knowing that you will always deliver me. Thank you for helping me to develop the character that produces hope.

TREASURES IN HEAVEN

"Don't store up treasures here on earth, where moths eat them and rust destroys them, and where thieves break in and steal. Store your treasures in heaven, where moths and rust cannot destroy, and thieves do not break in and steal."

MATTHEW 6:19-20 NLT

No matter how careful we are, or how diligent we gather, our earthly treasures cannot last for eternity. At the end of our life, we cannot keep any of them. Everything we've worked so hard for will fade away. Instead of storing up treasures here on earth, we should focus on storing treasures in heaven. When the focus of our lives is eternity, we will be greatly rewarded.

If you want to know what your true priorities are, look at the way you spend your money. A quick look at your finances will reveal your goals and values. You'll quickly see if you value earthly goods more than heavenly rewards. Ask God to help you shift your priorities. He will faithful how you how.

Father, I don't want to be bound up in the pursuit of wealth or material possessions. Instead, I want to store up treasures in heaven.

SPEAK BLESSINGS

"The LORD bless you and keep you;
the LORD make his face shine on you and be gracious to you;
the LORD turn his face toward you and give you peace."

NUMBERS 6:24-26 NIV

In biblical times, it was common for patriarchs to bless their children and grandchildren. When a father gave a blessing to his son, it was a great honor. Likewise, the absence of a blessing was considered a pronouncement of doom. Generational blessings are everywhere in the Word, but they aren't really something we see practiced today. We've lost sight of a lot of valuable and poignant traditions.

You can use your words and position to bless your children and grandchildren. Speak truth over them and pass on the blessings that the Lord has given you. Declare that you are proud of them and that your love for them is steady. Commission them to do the work of the Lord and let your words over them be life-giving and God honoring.

Father, give me the words to say to my grandchildren. I want to bless them pass on a legacy of truth.

FORGIVE OTHERS

"Love your enemies, do good to those who hate you, bless those who curse you, pray for those who mistreat you."

LUKE 6:27-28 NIV

We have all been mistreated at some point in our lives. Whether someone says a careless word or purposely slights us, we know how it feels to be hurt. In those moments, we get to choose whether we allow the painful words to replay in our minds, or we forgive and bless those who hurt us. When we continue to dwell on the pain, we become bitter, and our hearts become hard.

Jesus understands rejection. He knows what it is like to be hurt and deserted. When you are hurt, turn to the one who can relate to your pain. Let him comfort you and lead you toward forgiveness, just as he forgave his perpetrators. Don't hold on to unforgiveness. As you seek to keep your heart soft, God will meet you and give you the grace to forgive.

Jesus, help me to bless my enemies. Convict me when I am holding on to hurt and help me to keep my heart soft.

SAVIOR

A child will be born for us,
a son will be given to us,
and the government will be on his shoulders.
He will be named
Wonderful Counselor, Mighty God,
Eternal Father, Price of Peace.

ISAIAH 9:6 CSB

Jesus gave up his heavenly throne for us. He came to earth as a baby among his own creation. Despite being God, he came as a helpless infant who entrusted his care and upbringing to others.

On this Christmas day, we give him the best of our worship and praise because he is so very worthy. We celebrate Jesus' life and the love he offers us. We call him wonderful Counselor, Mighty God, Eternal Father, and Prince of Peace.

Today, take a moment to dwell on who Jesus is. Remember his great humility and the suffering he encountered. Each of the names mentioned in Isaiah speaks of his character and goodness. Remember all the times that he has counseled you, led you, loved you as a father, and brought you peace.

I praise you, wonderful Savior, my almighty King!

PRAY LIKE HIM

"Our Father in heaven,
hallowed be your name,
your kingdom come,
your will be done,
on earth as it is in heaven."

MATTHEW 6:9-10 NIV

Jesus gave his disciples a template for prayer. When we are unsure of how to pray, we can look at his example. He started by acknowledging who God was and agreeing with his promises. This is something we can do as we communicate with the Lord. We too can recognize his position and agree with what he is doing in the world.

Don't hesitate to pray because you feel your words are inadequate or you don't know what to say. Scripture is yours to use freely as you talk with God. When you pray Scripture, you can be confident that what you are saying is good and right. When your words align with God's, there is no doubt that will be answered.

Jesus, thank you for the guidance you give me in Scripture. Help me to rely on your Word when I pray.

CORNERSTONE

"Anyone who listens to my teaching and follows it is wise, like a person who builds a house on solid rock. Though the rain comes in torrents and the floodwaters rise and the winds beat against that house, it won't collapse because it is built on bedrock."

MATTHEW 7:24-25 NLT

When our life is built upon the truth of Scripture, we can be confident and secure. No matter what trials come, we won't be shaken because God is the foundation of all we do. If we are in Christ, we know that even if everything around us falls, we will stand in his strength. He is reliable, steady, and trustworthy.

Do you feel as though your life is stable? When trials come, do they knock you off your feet? If the answer to those questions is yes, it might be time to reevaluate the cornerstone of your life. Lean wholeheartedly on Jesus. Cast your cares upon him and surrender your anxieties. Make room for his presence in your life and trust that he will lead you well.

Jesus, you are everything to me. I want life to be built firmly on you.

SPEAK TRUTH

"These commandments that I give you today are to be on your hearts. Impress them on your children. Talk about them when you sit at home and when you walk along the road, when you lie down and when you get up."

DEUTERONOMY 6:6-7 NIV

God's Word is meant to infiltrate every aspect of our lives. We aren't meant to simply read it in our quiet time and then hope it impacts our life. Deuteronomy says to teach it to our children and talk about it when we sit, walk, and go to bed. In other words, our conversations should overflow with the deliberate discussion of truth. God wants us to be talking about him.

Even if you're not used to talking about God with others, it's never too late to start. Ask your adult children what they're learning at the moment. Repeat a scripture to your grandchild when it comes to mind. Ask a friend their opinion on a biblical concept. Slowly, as you do it more and more, you'll find yourself comfortable incorporating God's truth into your everyday conversations.

Father, I want your Word to impact every corner of my life. Help me to speak boldly and share with others.

PROTECT AND ADVOCATE

He will rescue the poor when they cry to him;
he will help the oppressed, who have no one to defend them.
He feels pity for the weak and the needy,
and he will rescue them.

PSALM 72:12-13 NLT

What a compassionate God we serve. When most kings honor the elite, the wealthy, and the strong, God looks out for the least of these. He positions himself as the provider, defender, and deliverer of the ones whom others shun, reject, and abuse. In the same way, we should be concerned with those who struggle financially, are marginalized, or suffer ridicule.

The way that you love others will have a direct impact on your family. When you are compassionate toward people who are difficult to love, you show your children and grandchildren what it looks like to reflect Christ to a hurting world. When you choose to be judgmental, harsh, or point your finger, you communicate that you are above those who have less. Let God continuously soften your heart toward the oppressed. Ask him his opinion, and he will readily share it.

Jesus, help me to protect and advocate for the oppressed. Help me to set a precedence in my family of caring for the least of these.

ABBA FATHER

You did not receive a spirit of slavery to fall back into fear. Instead, you received the Spirit of adoption, by whom we cry out, "Abba, Father!" The Spirit himself testifies together with our spirit that we are God's children.

ROMANS 8:15-16 CSB

As proud Grandmas, we eagerly pull out our phones to share pictures of our beautiful grandchildren. We could go on and on about their cute antics. We are enamored with them and want everyone to see and know that they are ours. This is a small glimpse of how God feels about us. He is proud of his beloved children.

When you are filled with affection for your grandchildren, remember that you too are a dearly beloved child. No matter your age, you are noticed and seen by your good Father. He is proud that you are his and is delighted to have you in his family. He is happy that you are his and wants you to experience love and belonging in his presence.

God, thank you for your fatherly love. I want to know fully that I am yours. Give me a greater understanding of the love and acceptance I have in you.

HIS FIRST

You were once darkness, but now you are light in the Lord. Live as children of the light.

EPHESIANS 5:8 NIV

No matter what roles we play in life, our mantle as children of the light should take precedence. Before we were sisters, mothers, wives, or grandmothers, we were children of God. Being part of his family is the greatest honor we will ever experience. It far surpasses even the greatest blessings we can experience on earth.

As the year ends, remember that you are dearly loved and fully accepted no matter what role you embody. You can love extravagantly as a grandmother because you were extravagantly loved first. Every good thing in your life stems from being adored by the creator of the universe. Praise him for all he's done and find your greatest fulfillment in walking alongside him.

Father, help me to walk as a child of the light. Thank you for loving me and accepting me into your family.